Charles Dickens

by Martin Fido

Lecturer in English
University of Leeds

LONDON
ROUTLEDGE & KEGAN PAUL
NEW YORK : HUMANITIES PRESS

First published 1968
by Routledge and Kegan Paul Ltd
Broadway House, 68-74 Carter Lane
London, E.C.4

Printed in Great Britain
by Northumberland Press Limited
Gateshead

SBN

SBN 7100 2953 5 (C)
SBN 7100 2952 7 (P)

The Profiles in Literature Series

This series is designed to provide the student of literature and the general reader with a brief and helpful introduction to the major novelists and prose writers in English, American and foreign literature.

Each volume will provide an account of an individual author's writing career and works, through a series of carefully chosen extracts illustrating the major aspects of the author's art. These extracts are accompanied by commentary and analysis, drawing attention to particular features of the style and treatment. There is no pretence, of course, that a study of extracts can give a sense of the works as a whole, but this selective approach enables the reader to focus his attention upon specific features, and to be informed in his approach by experienced critics and scholars who are contributing to the series.

The volumes will provide a particularly helpful and practical form of introduction to writers whose works are extensive or which present special problems for the modern reader, who can then proceed with a sense of his bearings and an informed eye for the writer's art.

An important feature of these books is the extensive reference list of the author's works and the descriptive list of the most useful biographies, commentaries and critical studies.

B.C.S

Contents

CONTENTS

Charles Dickens—his life and works

Today the novel is the dominant literary form, and the serious novelist is automatically regarded as being a serious artist. Yet, throughout the eighteenth century the novel was regarded by critics and commentators as a minor and suspect form, not really worthy of being considered art at all. The rise of the novel, in both popularity and esteem, during the nineteenth century was largely owing to the success of two novelists: Sir Walter Scott, whose serious reputation, established by the successful poetry he had written before turning his hand to the writing of novels, lent respectability to the fiction he produced: and Charles Dickens, whose enormous popular success penetrated to all levels of society, raised him from obscure and slightly disreputable antecedents to a high position among the eminent Victorians, and wrung from such suspicious intellectuals as Carlyle the grudging concession that prose fiction so entertaining deserved to be read.

Early career

John Dickens was a naval pay clerk at Portsea when his son Charles was born in 1812. John was an amiable man, whose total inability to live within his income caused Charles intense anxiety during his childhood, and left him with an unusual concern for financial stability that was to make the novelist a publisher's dream in his avid pursuit of high sales, but a publisher's nightmare for his touchy insistence that the lion's share of all profits realised by his books must be his.

In 1814 John Dickens was transferred to London, and in 1817 the family moved to Chatham. The Chatham-Rochester area was to be Dickens' final home, and to play its part as the setting of several of his books. He certainly preferred it to the London with which he is more normally associated.

In 1822 the family returned to London, but Charles remained at school in Chatham for a further year. When he rejoined the family in London, their financial straits were such that Charles's formal education was halted, and he was sent out to work, pasting labels on bottles in a blacking factory at Hungerford Stairs. The boy's humiliation at this step down from middle- to working-class life was acute: it was increased when, despite family economies, his father was arrested for debt and lodged in the Marshalsea Prison. The short period during which Charles was in lodgings and earning his own living while his family were shamefully, but comfortably, ensconced in the Marshalsea, profoundly influenced his development. Dependence on his own exertions, and a touchy pride in the talent which made him a gentleman in defiance of his background, were to be characteristics of the adult Dickens which owed much to the experiences of his childhood. More directly related to his writings, and equally connected with the blacking factory period, we find a persistent, often excessive, sympathy with deprived children in the novels, as well as a gift for creating fictional children of markedly independent character and for offering a child's view of the world to an adult audience.

A small legacy released John Dickens from prison after only three months, and when the Navy Pay Office was forced to discharge him (with a pension) as a former insolvent, he found employment on his brother-in-law's journal *The Mirror of Parliament*, and became a gallery reporter in the House of Commons. There was now money enough to send Charles to school for a further two years, and in 1827 the boy humbly started on a legal career, first as office-boy and then as clerk to a firm of solicitors. In his spare time he taught himself shorthand, and gained practice in using it as a legal reporter in Doctor's Commons (a sort of anachronistic predecessor of the Courts of Admiralty, Divorce and Probate). This experience led the bright young man to form a very poor opinion of the time-hallowed institutions of the law; increasingly, the tradition which is offered as a justification of many of the more august features of British life came to seem a fault rather than a virtue to Dickens.

While he was working on the fringes of the law Dickens fell in love for the first time. Maria Beadnell was the daughter of a banker who refused to let her become entangled with a penniless young clerk. Adversity combined with Dickens' passionate and idealistic temperament to give the affair a profound significance for him, and when, thirty years later, Maria crossed his path again, he eagerly arranged an assignation, naively ignoring the probability of thirty years of marriage and child-bearing having altered the slim adolescent girl he remembered.

In 1832 Dickens joined the staff of the *True Sun*, and joined his father in the gallery of the House of Commons to report the speeches on the Reform Bill. After working with his father for the *Mirror*, Dickens was employed by the *Morning Chronicle* which was setting up as a rival to the *Times*. He was now one of the finest shorthand reporters covering Parliament. Statesmen who demanded a picked man to produce fast and accurate transcripts of their speeches were amazed at Dickens' youth when he appeared. He, meanwhile, was amazed by the stupid pomposity of parliamentary warfare, and for the rest of his life was to hold the legislature in contempt, looking to private action and private charity for the most effective reforms of society.

In 1834 Dickens adopted the pen-name Boz (the family nickname for one of his brothers), and began writing short humorous 'Sketches' for various journals. These were sufficiently successful to be published in book form, with illustrations by George Cruikshank, whose reputation at this time far outshone that of Dickens. The book's success enabled its author to marry Catherine Hogarth, the daughter of a fellow-journalist. She bore him a large family before temperamental and intellectual incompatability led to their separation.

The reputation the *Sketches* earned Dickens also led to his being invited, in 1836, to write a connecting text for a monthly series of comic cockney sporting plates to be drawn by the popular artist Seymour. When the illustrator committed suicide in the early weeks of the publication Dickens was able to dictate the future course of the work, and developing beyond the fragmentary facetiousness of the early chapters, proved himself to have a remarkable genius for comic and farcical writing.

He exploited three main sources: the farcical situations beloved of eighteenth-century comic novelists together with the grotesque caricature practised by Smollett; eccentric and dialect verbal oddities, which his shorthand experience had taught him to observe; and unrealistic characters, situations and speeches which would nevertheless be accepted by theatre audiences as appropriate to staged representation. All his life, Dickens continued

4

to be indebted to these sources, though he far outstripped his literary origins.

The popularity of *Pickwick* rose to unprecedented heights, and Dickens suddenly found himself, at the age of twenty-four, the most famous novelist of his day, and the most popular novelist England had ever known. At his peak he would appear to have outsold even the sensational and pornographic fiction for the masses which normally overtopped the sales successes of the serious Victorian novelists. Dickens' childhood had been marred by poverty and social uncertainty; as a successful writer he was perpetually grateful to and conscious of the demands of the reading public which had lifted him to wealth and fame.

A subsidiary result of *Pickwick*'s success was that its form of publication, the monthly serial, remained for Dickens the way in which he wrote all his novels, and for the next fifty years other novelists also used this form, which had hitherto been kept mainly for reprints of eighteenth-century classics, pious tracts, or the raffish 'London Life' novels of Theodore Hook and Pierce Egan. Serialisation meant that Dickens' novels were necessarily episodic, with ramifying subplots to provide the minor climaxes and succession of incidents needed to sustain the reader's interrupted interest.

Before *Pickwick* was completed, Dickens embarked on *Oliver Twist*, a novel embodying two new features which were to remain characteristic of his work. It was, in the first place, an attack on a social abuse : the state of the workhouses and parish poor relief after the passing of the Poor Law of 1834. Dickens never hesitated to use his novels as vehicles for his social ideas, usually exhibiting the suffering endured by the innocent as a result of authoritarian heartlessness. He was not alone in using the novel as an instrument of propaganda, but the practice did not become really widespread until the 1840s.

Although he was not a systematic political thinker, Dickens was on the whole temperamentally opposed to established authority, and strongly sympathetic to the respectable poor. At the same time he objected to interfering or doctrinaire humanitarian activity.

Oliver Twist was also a sensational book, associated by reviewers with the 'Newgate novels' of Bulwer Lytton and Harrison Ainsworth. Dickens objected that, unlike the other Newgate novelists, he did not make heroes of his criminals, and it is true that to the end of his life he regarded crime with abhorrence, even fearing in later years that his own work for prison reform had been too far-reaching, and reversing his one-time abolitionist attitude to capital punishment. But he was fascinated by the evils he hated, and continued to find in lives and environments of vice and squalor subjects for his pen.

In 1839 Dickens started another of his literary activities, the conduct of journals of miscellanea, to contain, among other things, serialised novels. *Master Humphrey's Clock* was not particularly successful after *The Old Curiosity Shop* had been completed, and it was wound up with the conclusion of *Barnaby Rudge*. But the journals conducted by Dickens from 1850 until his death, *Household Words* and its successor *All the Year Round*, were notable successes. Here again Dickens' example was powerful in encouraging a Victorian mode of publication; other writers, notably Harrison Ainsworth and Douglas Jerrold, decided to capitalise on their established names by linking them with their own journals, rather than editing an established periodical for someone else as Bulwer (Lytton) had done for Colburn the publisher and as Dickens himself had done briefly for Bentley.

In 1842 Dickens visited America where *The Old Curiosity Shop* had enjoyed a great success. He was lionised and fêted generally, but suffered some public abuse for raising the vexed question of American pirate publication of European writers. The publication of his *American Notes* did not help. Like his *Pictures from Italy* (1846) it tended to show that while Dickens was capable of recognising individual institutions abroad that could not be matched in England, essentially he was an insular middle-class Briton, and quite incapable of responding with wholehearted sympathy to an alien culture.

By the 1850s Dickens was undisputably the doyen of English novelists, hailed by the general public and serious critics alike as a healthy comedian and an elevating moralist, whose praise of hearth and home was sound and respectable. It was, therefore, distressing to many of his admirers when the breakdown of his marriage became public in 1858. But this had its largest effect on his reputation seventy years later, when, in the 1930s, it was for the first time publicly suggested that Ellen Ternan, the young actress with whom Dickens had been infatuated at the time when he separated from his wife, had in fact subsequently become his mistress. The exact nature of their relationship is still in dispute; what cannot be disputed is that a new critical interest in Dickens coincided so closely with the new biographical suggestions that the two may well be seen as associated.

Increasingly, after his death, the Chestertonian optimistic Dickens, creator of Pickwickian innocence and laughter, had looked inartistic in method, and hopelessly lacking in subject matter that could engage sophisticated adult attention. Now, using the new biographical material, Edmund Wilson (in his essay *Dickens: the Two Scrooges*, was able to isolate light and dark currents in Dickens' work and parallel them with the phases of a manic-depressive cycle. Most opportunely it could be shown to the emotionally grim mid-twentieth century that there was a grim side to Dickens, revealed especially in those later works which had not particularly appealed to Chesterton.

Since then, criticism has fastened on to this serious side of Dickens, and has also discovered more evidence of a conscious aesthetic in his work than Chesterton would have approved, or Leslie Stephen believed possible in a writer whose popular vigour he despised.

'The Inimitable' was one of Dickens' nicknames in his own circle, and there is much truth in it. Successors may be found: popular sub-literature and boys' comics tried to imitate his verbal skills, but succeeded only in reproducing the facetiousness of his immaturity. A limited amount of more or less Dickensian comedy was produced by H. G. Wells, but there was never a real 'school of Dickens'. His grotesques were in themselves too daring; Evelyn Waugh, the last serious writer to use comic grotesques, never produced a character as successfully bold as Sairey Gamp or Squeers.

The darker and more psychologically introspective Dickens was observed and imitated by Dostoevsky. But an imitation with the comedy withdrawn and the sensational material pulled away from staginess went for long unrecognised, as it still goes unimitated, in England. Dickens' extraordinary powers coupled with an extraordinary lack of restraint make him unique. He is, as Lionel Trilling has said, one of the two greatest English novelists (Jane Austen being the other). His verbal virtuosity and human range mean that he, unlike Jane Austen, can reasonably be compared with Shakespeare. Only Sterne and James Joyce have exceeded his sense of the possibilities of typography and language.

Dickens towers over Victorian literature. The line of boisterous optimistic novels exploiting external appearances, and the comedy of visually and morally eccentric characters, started by Fielding, is closed by the magnitude
8

of Dickens' achievement. Any attempt to draw on the eighteenth-century comic novel since Dickens has looked hopelessly anticlimactic.

Later reputation

An examination of some of the recurrent objections to Dickens gives some evidence of his achievement. Few writers could be subjected to such a wide range of charges; it is an astonishing feat to have survived them.

The commonest objection to Dickens is that he is a sentimentalist. Undeniably he resorts to an exaggerated and distasteful pathos in the attempt to create moments of tragedy. His art owes much to the popular theatre, and the popular theatre of his day was heavily melo-dramatic.

It should be noted that the fault to be found with Dickens' treatment of suffering or dying children or artisans lies not so much in his insistence on the unhappiness of their situation; rather it is the intolerable quality of inadequate virtue which he invokes, expecting to make his scenes thereby the more moving, which actually makes them unbearable. To a Victorian audience, the notion that faultless children might, to the great distress of their parents and friends, be called through lingering death-beds to heaven, afforded some morbid spiritual satisfaction, and Dickens' big pathetic scenes had for them the quality of high tragedy. But less philosophically idealistic periods find it impossible to feel deeply moved by characters who passively and virtuously suffer without showing any of the normal weaknesses of common humanity, or any of the difficult and unsympathetic strengths of personality of the outstanding human being. Often in Dickens one finds that a character's predicament is well drawn—Florence Dombey, or Stephen Blackpool (*Hard Times*) are

9

good examples—and yet full sympathy for the character is hindered by the fact that he or she responds to all trials and temptations with a patient and outspokenly virtuous resignation that seems to owe more to a child's book of religious instruction than to either reality or an adult system of ethics. Dickens' determination to retain the sympathy of his contemporary audience for his heroes and heroines has lost him the interest of subsequent audiences.

It must, however, be noted that not all moments of pathos are marred in this way. In Dickens' later works, when, significantly, his popular audience had somewhat diminished, he found himself increasingly able to present heroes and heroines with a modicum of human weakness. And even in his early period he was able to present an entirely satisfactory pathos if it was not at the centre of his attention. The death of the settler's child in chapter XXXIII of *Martin Chuzzlewit*, where the primary aim is an attack on the exploitation of immigrants in America, is a good example of this.

Associated with this criticism of Dickens' sentimentality is the objection that his writing was superficial: it is argued that the buoyant optimism which won him his huge early audience was part of an inadequate vision of the world's harshness and complexity, and that he is unable to present anything but theatrical surfaces of characters without inwardness. This can be simply answered from the *Pickwick Papers*. Here, if anywhere, Dickens created a jolly world of feasting, comedy and harmless adventure, where the power of a benevolently used purse could dispel all unhappiness. And yet even here a note of impenetrable darkness was introduced when Mr. Pickwick discovered in the Fleet prison, misery beyond his power to relieve, and preferred dismal solitude to the contemplation of this spectacle.

Not only is this darkness present in Dickens' earliest and jolliest writing; as his career developed it increasingly impinged upon and overshadowed his fun, so that in his last three or four novels it is difficult to find a merely comic character untouched by some degree of gloom or horror.

As for the supposed superficiality of Dickens' characterisation, closer examination of the novels suggests increasingly that Dickens' simplicity is lifelike in concealing deep implications under a surface directness. The notorious praise of Victorian family life, with the happy and contented family as a reiterated image of all goodness, now looks more like an intuitive grasping at psychological truth than a comfortable bow to a conventional ethic. In the bullying yet fascinating theatrical villains we are more inclined to see an instinctive understanding of neurotic sado-masochistic behaviour than an indolent borrowing from a tired stage convention. This is not to deny that Dickens did lift conventions from the stage; but he informed them with new life, and we are forced to ask ourselves why readers who would scarcely spare a moment's attention to *East Lynne* can find themselves avidly reading the doings of such stagey monsters as Fagin and Sikes.

Further, it is important to stress that Dickens' frequent success in creating good times is a vital part of his artistic achievement. Fun can be had in life, and Dickens presents it with the delighted exaggeration of a great raconteur, the linguistic humour of an outstanding master of English prose, and a wealth of material detail which both adds to the comedy and roots it in an imagined reality.

Another objection frequently raised has been that Dickens' social criticism was somehow wrong. The researches of Humphry House and Philip Collins have gone a long way towards establishing the nature of Dickens' social and political attitudes. It is not for the critic to endorse or oppose these; rather we must observe that most frequently Dickens shows a truly remarkable skill in associating his observations of social abuses with his feeling for the quality of human life and the interplay of emotions in which social abuses are tolerated. If Dickens is to be compared with Shakespeare this is not from a simple feeling that he had the joviality to create bluff Falstaffian types; rather one feels that at his best Dickens had the insight to have created something like *Henry IV, Parts I and II*, with a powerful sense of such human qualities as warmth and coldness, dissipation and calculation, success and failure, as part of a larger total scene embracing political judgement and social consequence, as well as personal triumphs and tragedies.

Scheme of extracts

The selection of extracts which follows tries to bring together the features of Dickens' work discussed in the Introduction; and to demonstrate the reasons for the adverse criticism which has grown up around his work; to answer such criticism, where it can be answered, with conflicting evidence; to demonstrate the use he makes of particular skills gained as a theatre-goer and an observant journalist; and, very roughly, to show by ordering, how Dickens' early vitality developed into his mature talent. Although I have not hesitated to move an example of a particular technique or attitude to accompany related techniques or attitudes from a similar period of work so that there may be a loose continuity between sections, I have followed a rough chronology of periods (*Pickwick* to *Chuzzlewit*, *Dombey* to *Hard Times*, and *Tale of Two Cities* to *Our Mutual Friend*) to compensate for the chronological displacement of individual novels.

Dickens' early period is heavily represented. I do not disagree with the view that his late period has high gains in seriousness and a better defined profundity to its credit. But the finest writing of late Dickens still takes the form of irony; however near to despair his vision of the world became he never ceased to write comedy. A belief in Dickens' greatness as an artist must mean a love of Dickens' comedy; a love of the late Dickens must rest firmly on an understanding of the peculiar depth and sophistication which was already apparent in the early Dickens, and from which the late Dickens developed.

Comic action

The mainstay of Dickens' popularity and a major element of his greatness has always been his simple comedy; his sheer capacity to make his readers laugh. Although throughout his career there were times when Dickens used comedy to make serious points, there were always times when he wrote to be funny, and excluded almost any other purpose whatever.

Vincent Crummles, the manager of a travelling theatre company, has brought a visitor to watch a rehearsal.

I

As Mrs. Vincent Crummles recrossed back to the table, there bounded on to the stage from some mysterious inlet, a little girl in a dirty white frock with tucks up to the knees, short trousers, sandaled shoes, white spencer, pink gauze bonnet, green veil and curl-papers; who turned a pirouette, cut twice in the air, turned another pirouette, then, looking off at the opposite wing, shrieked, bounded forward to within six inches of the footlights, and fell into a beautiful attitude of terror, as a shabby gentleman in an old pair of buff slippers came in at one powerful slide, and chattering his teeth, fiercely brandished a walking-stick.

'They are going through the Indian Savage and the Maiden,' said Mrs. Crummles.

'Oh!' said the manager, 'the little ballet interlude. Very good, go on. A little this way, if you please, Mr. Johnson. That'll do. Now!'

The manager clapped his hands as a signal to proceed, and the savage, becoming ferocious, made a slide towards the maiden; but the maiden avoided him in six twirls, and came down, at the end of the last one, upon the very points of her toes. This seemed to make some impression upon the savage; for, after a little more ferocity and chasing of the maiden into corners, he began to relent, and stroked his face several times with his right thumb and four fingers, thereby intimating that he was struck with admiration of the maiden's beauty. Acting upon the impulse of this passion, he (the savage) began to hit himself severe thumps in the chest, and to exhibit other indications of being desperately in love, which being rather a prosy proceeding, was very likely the cause of the maiden's falling asleep; whether it was or no, asleep she did fall, sound as a church, on a sloping bank, and the savage perceiving it, leant his left ear to his left hand, and nodded sideways, to intimate to all whom it might concern that she *was* asleep, and no shamming. Being left to himself, the savage had a dance, all alone. Just as he left off, the maiden woke up, rubbed her eyes, got off the bank, and had a dance all alone too—such a dance that the savage looked on in ecstasy all the while, and when it was done, plucked from a neighbouring tree some botanical curiosity, resembling a small pickled cabbage, and offered it to the maiden, who at first wouldn't have it, but on the savage shedding tears relented. Then the savage jumped for joy; then the maiden jumped for rapture at the sweet smell of the pickled cabbage. Then the savage and the maiden danced violently together, and, finally, the savage dropped down on one knee, and the maiden stood

16

on one leg upon his other knee; thus concluding the ballet, and leaving the spectators in a state of pleasing uncertainty, whether she would ultimately marry the savage, or return to her friends.

Nicholas Nickleby, ch. 23

Characteristically Dickens achieves comedy by combining close observation of unusual modes of behaviour or curious material objects with an innocent highlighting of the incongruities by the use of inappropriate language or a deliberate misunderstanding of the purposes and motives of his characters. Thus he is at pains to describe the grubby little theatre girl precisely before fixing her with the inappropriately romantic title of 'the maiden'. The vision of a 'shabby gentleman in an old pair of buff slippers' coming in 'at one powerful slide' shows a quick and economical selection of characteristics at the same time realistic in a rehearsing actor and inappropriate to a savage. Our sense of the absurdity of the ballet is heightened by the narrator's refusal to allow us to overlook each movement; our attention is called to the separate balletic steps of the maiden and the comparatively unballetic movements of the savage; we infer that all these movements were distinguishable by their ineptitude, and are amused. Dickens overwillingly accepts the dramatic illusion in taking the savage's blows on the chest as normal indications of passion, and wilfully misunderstands in seeing the stage flower first as looking *like* a pickled cabbage, and thereafter describing it *as* one.

The incident is beautifully timed as part of a novel; the ballet is complete, and we do not feel disappointed of any fun, but at the same time it is short enough not to impede the novel as a whole.

Exuberant domestic optimism

Dickens' early popularity was enhanced by his tendency to write vigorously and humorously in praise of happy and secure family life. Dickensian jollifications, often in celebration of Christmas, appealed variously to nostalgic patriotism (they always seemed to look back to a not-too-distant past, even when first written), social security (class pleasures in the different strata of middle-class society were carefully differentiated by Dickens), a simple religious sense of 'loving thy neighbour', and a rather vinous common humanity.

Mr. Pickwick and his friends have gone to spend Christmas with the family at Dingley Dell in Kent, where Mr. Trundle is to marry a daughter of the house.

2

Mr. Pickwick was awakened early in the morning, by a hum of voices and pattering of feet, sufficient to arouse even the fat boy from his heavy slumbers. He sat up in bed, and listened. The female servants and female visitors were running constantly to and fro; and there were such multitudinous demands for warm water, such repeated outcries for needles and thread, and so many half-suppressed entreaties of 'Oh, do come and tie me, there's a dear!' that Mr. Pickwick in his innocence began to imagine that something dreadful must have occurred, when he grew more awake, and remembered the wedding. The occasion being an important one, he dressed himself with peculiar care, and descended to the breakfast room.

There were all the female servants in a brand-new uniform of pink muslin gowns with white bows in their caps, running about the house in a state of excitement and agitation, which it would be impossible to describe. The old lady was dressed out, in a brocaded gown, which had not seen the light for twenty years, saving and excepting such truant rays as had stolen through the chinks in the box in which it had been laid by, during the whole time. Mr. Trundle was in high feather and spirits, but a little nervous withal. The hearty old landlord was trying to look very cheerful and unconcerned, but failing signally in the attempt. All the girls were in tears and white muslin, except a select two or three, who were being honoured with a private view of the bride and bridesmaids, up stairs. All the Pickwickians were in the most blooming array; and there was a terrific roaring on the grass in front of the house, occasioned by all the men, boys, and hobbledehoys attached to the farm, each of whom had got a white bow in his button-hole, and all of whom were cheering with might and main : being incited thereto, and stimulated therein, by the precept and example of Mr. Samuel Weller, who had managed to become mighty popular already, and was as much at home as if he had been born on the land.

A wedding is a licensed subject to joke upon, but there really is no great joke in the matter after all; we speak merely of the ceremony, and beg it to be understood that we indulge in no hidden sarcasm upon a married life. Mixed up with the pleasure and joy of the occasion, are the many regrets at quitting home, the tears of parting between parent and child, the consciousness of leaving the dearest and kindest friends of the happiest portion of human life, to encounter its cares and troubles with others still untried, and little known—natural feelings which we would not render this chapter mournful by describing, and which we should be still more unwilling to be supposed to ridicule.

Let us briefly say, then, that the ceremony was performed by the old clergyman, in the parish church of Dingley Dell, and that Mr. Pickwick's name is attached to the register, still preserved in the vestry thereof; that the young lady with the black eyes signed her name in a very unsteady and tremulous manner; and that Lady Emily's signature, as the other bridesmaid, is nearly illegible; that it all went off in very admirable style; that the young ladies generally, thought it far less shocking than they expected; and that although the owner of the black eyes and the arch smile informed Mr. Winkle that she was sure she could never submit to anything so dreadful, we have the very best reasons for thinking she was mistaken. To all this, we may add, that Mr. Pickwick was the first who saluted the bride : and that in so doing, he threw over her neck a rich gold watch and chain, which no mortal eyes but the jeweller's had ever beheld before. Then the old church bell rang as gaily as it could, and they all returned to breakfast.

Pickwick Papers, ch. 28

The third paragraph of this extract gives a key to the popularity of this sort of writing in its own time, as well as the reservations that critics today may feel about the consciously jovial Dickens. Knowing that his subject is taken very seriously by his audience, Dickens is excessively apologetic in his insistence that he is not mocking marriage as such. Rather than explain that he 'indulges in no hidden sarcasm upon a married life' would he not have done better to omit the ambiguous sentence altogether? The licensed joker in Dickens should never have drawn attention to himself backing away from a subject too grave to be laughed at; by so doing he invites the reader to wonder whether his other jokes may not be in bad taste. Such a consideration rapidly makes clear that it is the unwonted solemnity rather than the normal joking which is out of place; Dickens' cautiously bride-and-groomless wedding is, like his merely superficially christian Christmases, tainted by an uneasy pomposity.

But if the emptiness at the centre makes the seriousness a little disconcerting, the good humour of the surroundings and the skill with which minor participants are drawn goes some way to compensate. A careful lack of enumeration of female servants and visitors at the beginning of the passage creates general bustle. Dickens' vocabulary and syntax, often made extraordinary for comic purposes, are here restrained to a normal colloquial level. With rare exceptions, the humour of the passage depends upon our prior knowledge of the persons described, and is friendly towards them. Thus Mr. Trundle is nervous because it is his wedding day; the language becomes a little more pretentious ('incited thereto, and stimulated therein') when Sam Weller is mentioned, quietly pointing up Sam's London sharpness as compared with the country servants ('men, boys and hobbledehoys'), just as 'Mr. Samuel Weller' as a designation mutedly insinuates Sam's high opinion of himself. When describing the archness of the black-eyed girl, Dickens' own narrative voice becomes arch—'we have the best reasons for thinking she was mistaken'—so that again there is no sting in his comment.

So well, indeed, are the possible satirical teeth of the comedy drawn in the actual description of the wedding, that Dickens' oily insistence that he has not mocked a sacred subject is quite a remarkable instance of the degree of obligation he felt to his readers.

Comic dialogue: monologue tradition

The actor Charles Mathews regularly performed solo, giving comic monologues and developing mannerisms whereby the characters he presented could be instantly recognised as unique personalities. Dickens attended his performances as a young man, and adapted his techniques to the novel. The vast majority of celebrated 'Dickens characters' are identified by tags and tricks of speech which they introduce in long monologue-like speeches, and then use throughout their later dialogue.

Mrs. Sairey Gamp, nurse and midwife, has dropped in on Mr. Mould the undertaker and his family for a little conversation.

3

'There are some happy creeturs,' Mrs. Gamp observed, 'as time runs back'ards with, and you are one, Mrs. Mould; not that he need do nothing except use you in his most owldacious way for years to come, I'm sure; for young you are and will be. I says to Mrs. Harris,' Mrs. Gamp continued, 'only t'other day; the last Monday evening fortnight as ever dawned upon this Piljian's Projiss of a mortal wale; I says to Mrs. Harris when she says to me, "Years
22

and our trials, Mrs. Gamp, sets marks upon us all."—"Say not the words, Mrs. Harris, if you and me is to be continual friends, for sech is not the case. Mrs. Mould," I says, making so free, I will confess, as use the name,' (she curtseyed here,) ' "is one of them that goes agen the obserwation straight; and never, Mrs. Harris, whilst I've a drop of breath to draw, will I set by, and not stand up, don't think it."—"I ast your pardon, ma'am," says Mrs. Harris, "and I humbly grant your grace; for if ever a woman lived as would see her feller creeturs into fits to serve her friends, well do I know that woman's name is Sairey Gamp."'

At this point she was fain to stop for breath; and advantage may be taken of the circumstance, to state that a fearful mystery surrounded this lady of the name of Harris, whom no one in the circle of Mrs. Gamp's acquaintance had ever seen; neither did any human being know her place of residence, though Mrs. Gamp appeared on her own showing to be in constant communication with her. There were conflicting rumours on the subject; but the prevalent opinion was that she was a phantom of Mrs. Gamp's brain—as Messrs. Doe and Roe are fictions of the law—created for the express purpose of holding visionary dialogues with her on all manner of subjects, and invariably winding up with a compliment to the excellence of her nature.

'And likeways what a pleasure,' said Mrs. Gamp, turning with a tearful smile towards the daughters, 'to see them two young ladies as I know'd afore a tooth in their pretty heads was cut, and have many a day seen—ah, the sweet creeturs!—playing at berryins down in the shop, and follerin' the order-book to its long home in the iron safe! But that's all past and over, Mr. Mould;' as she thus got in a carefully regulated routine to that gentleman, she shook her head waggishly; 'That's all past and over now, sir, an't it?'

'Changes, Mrs. Gamp, changes!' returned the undertaker.

'More changes too, to come, afore we've done with changes, sir,' said Mrs. Gamp, nodding yet more waggishly than before. 'Young ladies with such faces thinks of something else besides berryins, don't they, sir?'

'I am sure I don't know, Mrs. Gamp,' said Mould with a chuckle—'Not bad in Mrs. Gamp, my dear?'

'Oh yes, you do know, sir!' said Mrs. Gamp, 'and so does Mrs. Mould, your ansome pardner too, sir; and so do I, although the blessing of a daughter was deniged me; which, if we had one, Gamp would certainly have drunk its little shoes right off its feet, as with our precious boy he did, and arterwards send the child a errand to sell his wooden leg for any money it would fetch as matches in the rough, and bring it home in liquor; which was truly done beyond his years, for ev'ry individgle penny that child lost at toss or buy for kidney ones; and come home arterwards quite bold, to break the news, and offering to drown himself if sech would be a satisfaction to his parents. —Oh yes, you do know, sir,' said Mrs. Gamp, wiping her eye with her shawl, and resuming the thread of her discourse. 'There's something besides births and berryins in the newspapers, an't there, Mr. Mould?'

Mr. Mould winked at Mrs. Mould, whom he had by this time taken on his knee, and said : 'No doubt. A good deal more, Mrs. Gamp. Upon my life, Mrs. Gamp is very far from bad, my dear!'

'There's marryings, an't there, sir?' said Mrs. Gamp, while both the daughters blushed and tittered. 'Bless their precious hearts, and well they knows it! Well you know'd it too, and well did Mrs. Mould, when you was at their time of life! But my opinion is, you're all of one age now. For as to you and Mrs. Mould, sir, ever having grandchildren—'

'Oh! Fie, fie! Nonsense, Mrs. Gamp,' replied the undertaker. 'Devilish smart, though. Ca-pi-tal!' This was in a whisper. 'My dear'—aloud again—'Mrs. Gamp can drink a glass of rum, I dare say. Sit down, Mrs. Gamp, sit down.'

Mrs. Gamp took the chair that was nearest the door, and

24

casting up her eyes towards the ceiling, feigned to be wholly insensible to the fact of a glass of rum being in preparation, until it was placed in her hand by one of the young ladies, when she exhibited the greatest surprise.

'A thing,' she said, 'as hardly ever, Mrs. Mould, occurs with me unless it is when I am indispoged, and find my half a pint of porter settling heavy on the chest. Mrs. Harris often and often says to me, "Sairey Gamp," she says, "you raly do amaze me!" "Mrs. Harris," I says to her, "why so? Give it a name, I beg." "Telling the truth then ma'am," says Mrs. Harris, "and shaming him as shall be nameless betwixt you and me, never did I think till I know'd you, as any woman could sick-nurse and monthly likeways, on the little that you takes to drink." "Mrs. Harris," I says to her, "none on us knows what we can do till we tries; and wunst, when me and Gamp kept ouse, I thought so too. But now," I says, "my half a pint of porter fully satisfies; perwisin', Mrs. Harris, that it is brought reg'lar, and draw'd mild. Whether I sicks or monthlies, ma'am, I hope I does my duty, but I am but a poor woman, and I earns my living hard; therefore I *do* require it, which I makes confession, to be brought reg'lar and draw'd mild." '

Martin Chuzzlewit, ch. 25

Mrs. Gamp is made recognisable as a character by the furniture of her mind: Mrs. Harris, Gamp's wooden leg, and the references to life as a 'wale of tears' signal the personality of the speaker to the reader. So also does her unique habit of replacing *s* with *ge* ('dispoged'). More subtly, Mrs. Gamp, like Dickens' other grotesques, is given her own recognisable speech rhythm: in her case a matter of long rambling sentences in which the pauses for breath open up new and barely related clauses. Her non-repetitive mispronunciations are often chosen for visual effect: it is funnier to read 'Piljian's Projiss' from the page than to hear the words spoken, because the spelling Dickens has

25

chosen suggests first a mental confusion of Pilgrim and Christian which cannot easily be reproduced vocally, and secondly a notion of auditory attraction, *ji* following *ji* regardless of sense, which might be lost on a hearer who suspected Mrs. Gamp of merely visualising *Progress* without the *r*.

Notice how much of the effect is borrowed from theatrical technique. The whole passage turns easily into comic monologue; in later life Dickens himself made just such a monologue of Mrs. Gamp's major speeches. Alternately, Mr. Mould acts, now as a comic's feed, and now as an appreciative audience. (The popular theatre of Dickens' day, like the music-halls, could anticipate a moderate amount of unsolicited audience participation and comment.)

Mrs. Harris is funny as she stands, but notice that her existence as a phantom with whom Mrs. Gamp can hold imaginary conversation would be unremarkable if Mrs. Gamp were in fact a comedienne using an imaginary name as a catch-phrase in her act. By transporting theatrical conventions to the world of fictional reality Dickens found a new comic vein.

Social comedy

Dickens' interest in the structure of society was not re-
stricted to indignation over social problems. He enjoyed
the harmless human foibles exposed and canalised by the
class system, and laughed as pleasantly at harmless snob-
beries and meannesses as he laughed angrily at larger and
more dangerous examples of the same vices. When dis-
playing a group of characters from the same stratum of
society he could make the group itself take on an almost
unanimous personality, yet with no sacrifice of comic
by-play between individuals.

Newman Noggs, a reduced gentleman, has informed his
fellow-lodger Crowl that he has been invited to dinner
with other tenants in their building, whom Crowl assumes
to be the 'Kenwigses'.

4

The lodgers to whom Crowl had made allusion under
the designation of the 'Kenwigses', were the wife and
olive branches of one Mr. Kenwigs, a turner in ivory,
who was looked upon as a person of some consideration on
the premises, inasmuch as he occupied the whole of the

first floor, comprising a suite of two rooms. Mrs. Kenwigs, too, was quite a lady in her manners, and of a very genteel family, having an uncle who collected a water-rate; besides which distinction, the two eldest of her little girls went twice a week to a dancing school in the neighbourhood, and had flaxen hair, tied with blue ribands, hanging in luxuriant pigtails down their backs; and wore little white trousers with frills round the ancles—for all of which reasons, and many more equally valid but too numerous to mention, Mrs. Kenwigs was considered a very desirable person to know, and was the constant theme of all the gossips in the street, and even three or four doors round the corner at both ends.

It was the anniversary of that happy day on which the church of England as by law established, had bestowed Mrs. Kenwigs upon Mr. Kenwigs; and in grateful commemoration of the same, Mrs. Kenwigs had invited a few select friends to cards and a supper in the first floor, and had put on a new gown to receive them in: which gown, being of a flaming colour and made upon a juvenile principle, was so successful that Mr. Kenwigs said the eight years of matrimony and five children seemed all a dream, and Mrs. Kenwigs younger and more blooming than on the very first Sunday he had kept company with her.

Beautiful as Mrs. Kenwigs looked when she was dressed though, and so stately that you would have supposed she had a cook and housemaid at least, and nothing to do but order them about, she had a world of trouble with the preparations; more, indeed, than she, being of a delicate and genteel constitution, could have sustained, had not the pride of housewifery upheld her. At last, however, all the things that had to be got together were got together, and all the things that had to be got out of the way were got out of the way, and everything was ready, and the collector himself having promised to come, fortune smiled upon the occasion.

The party was admirably selected. There were, first of

28

all, Mr. Kenwigs and Mrs. Kenwigs, and four olive Kenwigses who sat up to supper; firstly, because it was but
right that they should have a treat on such a day; and
secondly, because their going to bed, in presence of the
company, would have been inconvenient, not to say
improper. Then, there was a young lady who had made
Mrs. Kenwigs's dress, and who—it was the most convenient thing in the world—living in the two-pair back,
gave up her bed to the baby, and got a little girl to watch
it. Then, to match this young lady, was a young man,
who had known Mr. Kenwigs when he was a bachelor, and
was much esteemed by the ladies as bearing the reputation
of a rake. To these, were added a newly-married couple,
who had visited Mr. and Mrs. Kenwigs in their courtship;
and a sister of Mrs. Kenwigs's, who was quite a beauty;
besides whom, there was another young man, supposed to
entertain honourable designs upon the lady last mentioned; and Mr. Noggs, who was a genteel person to ask,
because he had been a gentleman once. There were also
an elderly lady from the back parlour, and one more
young lady, who, next to the collector, perhaps, was the
great lion of the party, being the daughter of a theatrical
fireman, who 'went on' in the pantomime, and had the
greatest turn for the stage that was ever known, being
able to sing and recite in a manner that brought tears into
Mrs. Kenwigs's eyes. There was only one drawback upon
the pleasure of seeing such friends, and that was that the
lady in the back-parlour, who was very fat, and turned of
sixty, came in a low book-muslin dress and short kid
gloves, which so exasperated Mrs. Kenwigs, that the lady
assured her visitors, in private, that if it hadn't happened
that the supper was cooking at the back-parlour grate at
that moment, she certainly would have requested its
representative to withdraw.

'My dear,' said Mr. Kenwigs, 'wouldn't it be better to
begin a round game?'

'Kenwigs, my dear,' returned his wife, 'I am surprised
at you. Would you begin without my uncle?'

'I forgot the collector,' said Kenwigs; 'oh no, that would never do.'

'He's so particular,' said Mrs. Kenwigs, turning to the other married lady, 'that if we began without him, I should be out of his will for ever.'

'Dear!' cried the married lady.

'You've no idea what he is,' replied Mrs. Kenwigs; 'and yet as good a creature as ever breathed.'

'The kindest-hearted man as ever was,' said Kenwigs.

'It goes to his heart, I believe, to be forced to cut the water off, when the people don't pay,' observed the bachelor friend, intending a joke.

'George,' said Mr. Kenwigs, solemnly, 'none of that, if you please.'

'It was only my joke,' said the friend, abashed.

'George,' rejoined Mr. Kenwigs, 'a joke is a wery good thing—a wery good thing—but when that joke is made at the expense of Mrs. Kenwigs's feelings, I set my face against it. A man in public life expects to be sneered at—it is the fault of his elewated sitiwation, and not of himself. Mrs. Kenwigs's relation is a public man, and that he knows, George, and that he can bear; but putting Mrs. Kenwigs out of the question (if I *could* put Mrs. Kenwigs out of the question on such an occasion as this), I have the honour to be connected with the collector by marriage; and I cannot allow these remarks in my—' Mr. Kenwigs was going to say 'house', but he rounded the sentence with 'apartments'.

At the conclusion of these observations, which drew forth evidences of acute feeling from Mrs. Kenwigs, and had the intended effect of impressing the company with a deep sense of the collector's dignity, a ring was heard at the bell.

'That's him,' whispered Mr. Kenwigs, greatly excited. 'Morleena, my dear, run down and let your uncle in, and kiss him directly you get the door open. Hem! Let's be talking.'

Adopting Mr. Kenwigs's suggestion, the company spoke

very loudly, to look easy and unembarrassed; and almost as soon as they had begun to do so, a short old gentleman in drabs and gaiters, with a face that might have been carved out of *lignum vitae*, for anything that appeared to the contrary, was led playfully in, by Miss Morleena Kenwigs, regarding whose uncommon Christian name it may be here remarked that it had been invented and composed by Mrs. Kenwigs previous to her first lying-in, for the special distinction of her eldest child, in case it should prove a daughter.

Nicholas Nickleby, ch. 14

The title of the chapter from which this extract is taken is *Having the Misfortune to treat of none but common people, is necessarily of a mean and vulgar character.* Thus the joke works back to the reader, for can we, after that, fail to recognise that we too are guilty of petty snobbery if we feel ourselves to be superior to the Kenwigses?

The interest in status is supreme; the carpet slippers of the 'savage' in Mr. Crummles' ballet were merely an incongruity for a dancer; the 'low book-muslin dress and short kid gloves' of the old lady from the back parlour are only of interest insofar as they represent a social gaffe. With fascinated precision Dickens outlines the class limits of a group which demands some pretension to 'gentility' from all its members, and regards a water-rate collector as an important public servant.

The concentration on this precision for comic effect means that Dickens here feels no need to explain laboriously that he is not attacking family life as such when he laughs at the formalities of the Kenwigs's anniversary celebrations. It is clear enough that the Kenwigs's family loyalty is inherently a good thing, although its manifestation in a concern to wring legacies from the rate-collecting uncle is a human failing. Equally clearly, moral comment is not Dickens' point.

It is worth noting Dickens' rejection of abstract writing to achieve his results. Instead of naming the social station of the Kenwigses, or assessing the incomes of the members of the party, he shows us what possessions they have, and leaves us to draw our own conclusions.

Dickens has been accused of being an unnecessarily long-winded writer, and yet his digressions are not purposeless. Notice, for example, how the apparently unnecessary suggestion that Mrs. Kenwigs when dressed looked like the mistress of a cook and housemaid actually insinuates an ideal dream of the group portrayed: they would like to have nothing to do but order servants about.

Social satire: caricature and irony

Throughout his life Dickens was interested in public affairs, and although his popular reputation may, to some extent, have exaggerated the progressive or radical quality of his thinking, he certainly did write forcibly against a number of official abuses, and, by and large, was regarded throughout his lifetime as a friend of the poor, and a dangerous enemy to certain types of public servant.

Mr. Bumble the beadle has just posted a notice advertising that £5 will be given to any tradesman accepting the parish boy, Oliver Twist, as an apprentice, when he falls into conversation with Mr. Sowerberry the undertaker.

5

'By the bye,' said Mr. Bumble, 'you don't know anybody who wants a boy, do you? A porochial 'prentice, who is at present a dead-weight; a millstone, as I may say; round the porochial throat? Liberal terms, Mr. Sowerberry, liberal terms!' As Mr. Bumble spoke, he raised his cane to the bill above him, and gave three distinct raps upon the words 'five pounds:' which were printed thereon in Roman capitals of gigantic size.

'Gadso!' said the undertaker: taking Mr. Bumble by the gilt-edged lappel of his official coat; 'that's just the very thing I wanted to speak to you about. You know—dear me, what a very elegant button this is, Mr. Bumble! I never noticed it before.'

'Yes, I think it is rather pretty,' said the beadle, glancing proudly downwards at the large brass buttons which embellished his coat. 'The die is the same as the porochial seal—the Good Samaritan healing the sick and bruised man. The board presented it to me on New-year's morning, Mr. Sowerberry. I put it on, I remember, for the first time, to attend the inquest on that reduced tradesman, who died in a doorway at midnight.'

'I recollect,' said the undertaker. 'The jury brought in, "Died from exposure to the cold, and want of the common necessities of life," didn't they?'

Mr. Bumble nodded.

'And they made it a special verdict, I think,' said the undertaker, 'by adding some words to the effect, that if the relieving officer had—'

'Tush! Foolery!' interposed the beadle. 'If the board attended to all the nonsense that ignorant jurymen talk, they'd have enough to do.'

'Very true,' said the undertaker; 'they would indeed.'

'Juries,' said Mr. Bumble, grasping his cane tightly, as was his wont when working into a passion: 'juries is ineddicated, vulgar, grovelling wretches.'

'So they are,' said the undertaker.

'They haven't no more philosophy nor political economy about 'em than that,' said the beadle, snapping his fingers contemptuously.

'No more they have,' acquiesced the undertaker.

'I despise 'em,' said the beadle, growing very red in the face.

'So do I,' rejoined the undertaker.

'And I only wish we had a jury of the independent sort,

34

in the house for a week or two,' said the beadle; 'the rules and regulations of the board would soon bring their spirit down for 'em.'

'Let 'em alone for that,' replied the undertaker. So saying, he smiled, approvingly: to calm the rising wrath of the indignant parish officer.

Mr. Bumble lifted off his cocked hat; took a handkerchief from the inside of the crown; wiped from his forehead the perspiration which his rage had engendered; fixed the cocked hat on again; and, turning to the undertaker, said in a calmer voice:

'Well; what about the boy?'

'Oh!' replied the undertaker; 'why, you know, Mr. Bumble, I pay a good deal towards the poor's rates.'

'Hem!' said Mr. Bumble. 'Well?'

'Well,' replied the undertaker, 'I was thinking that if I pay so much towards 'em, I've a right to get as much out of 'em as I can, Mr. Bumble; and so—and so—I think I'll take the boy myself.'

Mr. Bumble grasped the undertaker by the arm, and led him into the building. Mr. Sowerberry was closeted with the board for five minutes; and it was arranged that Oliver should go to him that evening 'upon liking,'—a phrase which means, in the case of a parish apprentice, that if the master find, upon a short trial, that he can get enough work out of a boy without putting too much food into him, he shall have him for a term of years, to do what he likes with.

Oliver Twist, ch. 4

Blatant hyperbole is normal in Dickens' early satire. As potentially real people Bumble and Sowerberry are incredible: no one could be so insensitive as to refer immediately to an occasion giving the lie to the emblem of which he is boasting, as Bumble does; or gauchely lead the conversation to a point of one's companion's public humiliation, as Sowerberry does; or openly reveal the evils of the system he represents with malevolent pride, as Bumble does in his wishes for jurors. But these implausibilities serve to expose what Dickens believes to be the real attitudes underlying the inhumanity of parish Boards of Guardians and their employees.

Ironies abound. Bumble's mispronunciations undercut the dignity of parish office with which he seeks to invest himself, and destroy his own pretensions to education. The design of the parish seal is almost crude in its direct comment on the gap between the board's supposed purpose and actual achievement. Sowerberry's acquiescence in Bumble's remarks on juries' ignorance carries the double weight of intentional agreement with Bumble's spirit, and an accidental confirmation of the actual verbal statements which can be drawn from Bumble's sarcasms—(i.e. it would be a *good* thing if boards did more, and it *is* a good thing that jurors know nothing of political economy).

Comic villains: melodrama tradition

Until the middle of his career, Dickens' treatment of evil was strongly theatrical, and, in the tradition of his time, this meant that villains were stereotyped monsters whose unrelieved wickedness was not without its comic aspect. It was one of Dickens' greatest achievements to exploit this comedy to the full while at the same time suggesting an unusual degree of psychological sickness. The theatre's unreality of exaggeration became, in his hands, an unreality akin to hallucination.

With the help of his sister Sally, Sampson Brass, a rascally attorney, has carried out the orders of the malignant dwarf, Daniel Quilp, and has had Quilp's honest enemy, Kit Nubbles, committed for trial, charged with a theft he did not commit. On a visit to the lonely wharf where Quilp has his office, Brass is alarmed to overhear Quilp chanting extracts from the newspaper account of the proceedings before the magistrates as a triumphal song. He is still more startled by what he sees.

6

All this time, Sampson was rubbing his hands and staring,

with ludicrous surprise and dismay, at a great, goggle-eyed, blunt-nosed figure-head of some old ship, which was reared up against the wall in a corner near the stove, looking like a goblin or hideous idol whom the dwarf worshipped. A mass of timber on its head, carved into the dim and distant semblance of a cocked hat, together with a representation of a star on the left breast and epaulettes on the shoulders, denoted that it was intended for the effigy of some famous admiral; but, without those helps, any observer might have supposed it the authentic portrait of a distinguished merman, or great sea-monster. Being originally much too large for the apartment which it was now employed to decorate, it had been sawn off short at the waist. Even in this state it reached from floor to ceiling; and thrusting itself forwards with that excessively wide-awake aspect, and air of somewhat obtrusive politeness, by which figureheads are usually characterised, seemed to reduce everything else to mere pigmy proportions.

'Do you know it?' said the dwarf, watching Sampson's eyes. 'Do you see the likeness?'

'Eh?' said Brass, holding his head on one side, and throwing it a little back, as connoisseurs do. 'Now I look at it again, I fancy I see a—yes, there certainly is something in the smile that reminds me of—and yet upon my word I—'

Now, the fact was, that Sampson, having never seen anything in the smallest degree resembling this substantial phantom, was much perplexed; being uncertain whether Mr. Quilp considered it like himself, and had therefore bought it for a family portrait; or whether he was pleased to consider it as the likeness of some enemy. He was not very long in doubt; for, while he was surveying it with that knowing look which people assume when they are contemplating for the first time portraits which they ought to recognise but don't, the dwarf threw down the newspaper from which he had been chanting the words already quoted, and seizing a rusty iron bar, which he used in lieu of a poker, dealt the figure such a stroke on the nose that it rocked again.

'Is it like Kit—is it his picture, his image, his very self?' cried the dwarf, aiming a shower of blows at the insensible countenance, and covering it with deep dimples. 'Is it the exact model and counterpart of the dog—is it—is it—is it?' And with every repetition of the question, he battered the great image until perspiration streamed down his face with the violence of the exercise.

Although this might have been a very comical thing to look at from a secure gallery, as a bull-fight is found to be a comfortable spectacle by those who are not in the arena, and a house on fire is better than a play to people who don't live near it, there was something in the earnestness of Mr. Quilp's manner which made his legal adviser feel that the counting-house was a little too small, and a great deal too lonely, for the due enjoyment of these humours. Therefore he stood as far off as he could while the dwarf was thus engaged; whimpering out but feeble applause; and when he left off and sat down again from pure exhaustion, approached with more obsequiousness than ever.

'Excellent indeed!' cried Brass. 'He he! Oh, very good, sir. You know,' said Sampson, looking round as if in appeal to the bruised admiral, 'he's quite a remarkable man—quite!'

'Sit down,' said the dwarf. 'I bought the dog yesterday. I've been screwing gimlets into him, and sticking forks in his eyes, and cutting my name on him. I mean to burn him at last.'

'Ha ha!' cried Brass. 'Extremely entertaining, indeed!'

'Come here!' said Quilp, beckoning him to draw near. 'What's injudicious, hey?'

'Nothing, sir—nothing. Scarcely worth mentioning, sir; but I thought that song—admirably humorous in itself you know—was perhaps rather—'

'Yes,' said Quilp, 'rather what?'

'Just bordering, or as one might say remotely verging

39

upon the confines of injudiciousness perhaps, sir,' returned Brass, looking timidly at the dwarf's cunning eyes, which were turned towards the fire and reflected its red light.

'Why?' inquired Quilp, without looking up.

'Why, you know, sir,' returned Brass, venturing to be more familiar: '—the fact is, sir, that any allusion to these little combinings together of friends for objects in themselves extremely laudable, but which the law terms conspiracies, are—you take me, sir?—best kept snug and among friends, you know.'

'Eh!' said Quilp, looking up with a perfectly vacant countenance. 'What do you mean?'

'Cautious, exceedingly cautious, very right and proper!' cried Brass, nodding his head. 'Mum, sir, even here—my meaning, sir, exactly.'

'*Your* meaning exactly, you brazen scarecrow,—what's your meaning?' retorted Quilp. 'Why do you talk to me of combining together? Do *I* combine? Do *I* know anything about your combining?'

'No no, sir—certainly not; not by any means,' returned Brass.

'If you so wink and nod at me,' said the dwarf, looking about him as if for his poker, 'I'll spoil the expression of your monkey's face, I will.'

'Don't put yourself out of the way I beg, sir,' rejoined Brass, checking himself with great alacrity. 'You're quite right, sir, quite right. I shouldn't have mentioned the subject, sir. It's much better not to. You're quite right, sir. Let us change it, if you please. You were asking, sir, Sally told me, about our lodger. He has not returned, sir.'

'No?' said Quilp, heating some rum in a little saucepan, and watching it to prevent its boiling over. 'Why not?'

'Why, sir,' returned Brass, 'he—dear me, Mr. Quilp, sir—'

'What's the matter?' said the dwarf, stopping his hand in the act of carrying the saucepan to his mouth.

'You have forgotten the water, sir,' said Brass, 'And—excuse me, sir—but it's burning hot.'

40

Deigning no other than a practical answer to this remonstrance, Mr. Quilp raised the hot saucepan to his lips, and deliberately drank off all the spirit it contained, which might have been in quantity about half a pint, and had been but a moment before, when he took it off the fire, bubbling and hissing fiercely. Having swallowed this gentle stimulant, and shaken his fist at the admiral, he bade Mr. Brass proceed.

The Old Curiosity Shop, ch. 62

In all externals, Quilp has stepped straight from the popular lowbrow theatre: he is villainously deformed; hatred and suspicion are his most characteristic emotions, and he expresses them without reserve; his tastes, as exemplified in the boiling rum, are unnatural and alarming; and other characters, even evil accomplices like Sampson Brass, visibly cower before him.

But Dickens carries into this stock picture of unmitigated malice a genuinely powerful suggestion of obsessively compulsive behaviour. Quilp's action in beating the figurehead, his repetitive questions and his final account of his use of and intentions for the vast block of wood which stands for his enemy are all simply insane. We are not meant to miss this point; Sampson Brass's fear of his accomplice while he beats the figurehead is contrasted with the security of those who watch enraged (irrational) bulls from the safety of a spectators' gallery, and it is 'something in the earnestness of Mr. Quilp's manner' i.e., the fact that Mr. Quilp sees lambasting and abusing a figurehead as a perfectly reasonable and serious occupation, rather than the evil nature of his motives, which makes Brass uneasy about sharing a small room with him. Psychological stress and abnormality were matters of lifelong interest to Dickens; he can expose and use them in the most unlikely circumstances.

Unlikely, because Quilp is also a great comic character.

41

The use of his beating a figurehead as a suggestion of his underlying dangerous insanity should not conceal from us the absurdity of the whole incident. Dickens is acutely aware of this, making fun of the figurehead's absurdity, and the impossibility of its looking even like the admiral for whom it was intended to normal eyes. Our alarm at a character who enjoys torturing a piece of wood is mitigated by our amusement at his specifying that he has done it with 'forks' and 'gimlets'. Like Dickens' other great comic figures, Quilp's dialogue has a characteristic rhythm; the short jerky phrases and sentences which start with the same word in sequence, and rise quickly to a concluding climax.

Serious dialogue: melodrama tradition

Dickens' passion for the theatre was not always a blessing. Particularly in his early work it gave him a tendency to create stereotyped characters uttering melodramatic verbiage in dully conventional moments of high drama.

Mr. Haredale, believing that young Edward Chester may share the depravity of his father, Sir John Chester, has connived at the deception whereby Sir John has kept Edward away from Haredale's niece and ward, Emma. Edward having now proved himself worthy, Mr. Haredale accepts that the lovers should be re-united.

7

'You are frank, honourable, and disinterested,' said Mr. Haredale; 'you have forced the conviction that you are so, even on my once-jaundiced mind, and I believe you. Wait here till I come back.'

He left the room as he spoke; but soon returned with his niece.

'On that first and only time,' he said, looking from the one to the other, 'when we three stood together under her father's roof, I told you to quit it, and charged you never to return.'

'It is the only circumstance arising out of our love,' observed Edward, 'that I have forgotten.'

'You own a name,' said Mr. Haredale, 'I had deep reason to remember. I was moved and goaded by recollections of personal wrong and injury, I know, but, even now I cannot charge myself with having, then, or ever, lost sight of a heartfelt desire for her true happiness; or with having acted—however much I was mistaken—with any other impulse than the one pure, single, earnest wish to be to her, as far as in my inferior nature lay, the father she had lost.'

'Dear uncle,' cried Emma, 'I have known no parent but you. I have loved the memory of others, but I have loved you all my life. Never was father kinder to his child than you have been to me, without the interval of one harsh hour, since I can first remember.'

'You speak too fondly,' he answered, 'and yet I cannot wish you less partial; for I have a pleasure in hearing those words, and shall have in calling them to mind when we are far asunder, which nothing else could give me. Bear with me for a moment longer, Edward, for she and I have been together many years; and although I believe that in resigning her to you I put the seal upon her future happiness, I find it needs an effort.'

He pressed her tenderly to his bosom, and after a minute's pause, resumed:

'I have done you wrong, sir, and I ask your forgiveness—in no common phrase, or show of sorrow; but with earnestness and sincerity. In the same spirit, I acknowledge to you both that the time has been when I connived at treachery and falsehood—which if I did not perpetrate myself, I still permitted—to rend you two asunder.'

'You judge yourself too harshly,' said Edward. 'Let these things rest.'

'They rise up in judgement against me when I look back, and not now for the first time,' he answered. 'I cannot part from you without your full forgiveness; for busy life and I have little left in common now, and I have

44

regrets enough to carry into solitude, without addition to the stock.'

'You bear a blessing from us both,' said Emma. 'Never mingle thoughts of me—of me who owe you so much love and duty—with anything but undying affection and gratitude for the past, and bright hopes for the future.'

'The future,' returned her uncle, with a melancholy smile, 'is a bright word for you, and its image should be wreathed with cheerful hopes. Mine is of another kind, but it will be one of peace, and free, I trust, from care or passion. When you quit England I shall leave it too. There are cloisters abroad; and now that the two great objects of my life are set at rest, I know no better home. You droop at that, forgetting that I am growing old, and that my course is nearly run. Well, we will speak of it again—not once or twice, but many times; and you shall give me cheerful counsel, Emma.'

'And you will take it?' asked his niece.

'I'll listen to it,' he answered, with a kiss, 'and it will have its weight, be certain. What have I left to say? You have, of late, been much together. It is better and more fitting that the circumstances attendant on the past, which wrought your separation, and sowed between you suspicion and distrust, should not be entered on by me.'

'Much, much better,' whispered Emma.

'I avow my share in them,' said Mr. Haredale, 'though I held it at the time, in detestation. Let no man turn aside, ever so slightly, from the broad path of honour, on the plausible pretence that he is justified by the goodness of his end. All good ends can be worked out by good means. Those that cannot, are bad; and may be counted so at once, and left alone.'

He looked from her to Edward, and said in a gentler tone :

'In goods and fortune you are now nearly equal. I have been her faithful steward, and to that remnant of a richer property which my brother left her, I desire to add, in token of my love, a poor pittance, scarcely worth the

45

mention, for which I have no longer any need. I am glad you go abroad. Let our ill-fated house remain the ruin it is. When you return, after a few thriving years, you will command a better, and a more fortunate one. We are friends.'

Edward took his extended hand, and grasped it heartily.

'You are neither slow nor cold in your response,' said Mr. Haredale, doing the like by him, 'and when I look upon you now, and know you, I feel that I would choose you for her husband. Her father had a generous nature, and you would have pleased him well. I give her to you in his name, and with his blessing. If the world and I part in this act, we part on happier terms than we have lived for many a day.'

Barnaby Rudge, ch. 79

This scene as a whole has no intrinsic interest; it is merely a formal clearing away of the barriers which have stood between the lovers, and a dismissal of the now un-needed Mr. Haredale from their lives. There is neither effective presentation nor serious investigation of the emotions which purport to be depicted. The language is stilted and stale; the action described (past treachery; future retirement to a monastery) is stagey, and the speech rhythms constantly slip into a crude blank verse :

E : Never was a father kinder to his child
     Than you have been to me, without the interval
     Of one harsh hour, since I can first remember.

H : You speak too fondly, and yet I cannot wish
     You were less partial; for I have a pleasure
     In hearing those words.

It is unlikely that Dickens, who was capable of laughing uproariously at unconvincing conventions in the theatre, recognised that he was at this point lifting his account of human behaviour from his observation of the stage rather than his observation of life: one must remember the strange hold that literary stereotypes may exercise over society. After 100 years in which melodrama, or absurdly lofty drama, had taken the place of tragedy in the theatre, Victorian theatregoers probably believed that high emotions and passions *naturally* found expression in a language that suggests very debased Jacobean drama. And in the absence of sexual explicitness, Victorian readers welcomed a lack of verbal inhibition when passion was being presented. Once in the century the result was *Wuthering Heights*—a misunderstood failure with its contemporary audience. Sterile verbiage was what the Victorians wanted when love was under discussion: it is tempting to accuse our great-grandparents of emotional cowardice, and leave it at that, but in fairness to them it should be observed that nearly all periods have shown their areas of literary inhibition, and certainly the arts of today are not without sentimental and simplifying distortions that evade moral and emotional problems inherent in life as cosily as Dickens' absurd treatment of love in much of his early work protected his readers from coming to grips with such genuine questions as the relation of parental authority to parental love, or the value of sexuality in an amatory relationship.

Description of place: sensational horror

Dickens was slow in developing an art of restraint; from the popular theatre and his own natural vigour he derived the tendency towards an art of strong assertion, risking over-assertion, which he never entirely lost. Thus places in Dickens are likely to be described as extremes; idyllic rural scenes are exaggeratedly, and often unrealistically, perfect; town scenes have a greater life, of animation or corruption, than one supposes any real urban setting can ever have had.

Toby Crackit and Mr. Chitling are minor members of a criminal gang.

8

Near to that part of the Thames on which the church at Rotherhithe abuts, where the buildings on the banks are dirtiest and the vessels on the river blackest with the dust of colliers and the smoke of close-built low-roofed houses, there exists, at the present day, the filthiest, the strangest, the most extraordinary of the many localities that are hidden in London, wholly unknown, even by name, to the great mass of its inhabitants.

To reach this place, the visitor has to penetrate through a maze of close, narrow, and muddy streets, thronged by the roughest and poorest of water-side people, and devoted to the traffic they may be supposed to occasion. The cheapest and least delicate provisions are heaped in the shops; the coarsest and commonest articles of wearing apparel dangle at the salesman's door, and stream from the house-parapet and windows. Jostling with unemployed labourers of the lowest class, ballast-heavers, coal-whippers, brazen women, ragged children, and the very raff and refuse of the river, he makes his way with difficulty along, assailed by offensive sights and smells from the narrow alleys which branch off on the right and left, and deafened by the clash of ponderous waggons that bear great piles of merchandise from the stacks of warehouses that rise from every corner. Arriving, at length, in streets remoter and less-frequented than those through which he has passed, he walks beneath tottering house-fronts projecting over the pavement, dismantled walls that seem to totter as he passes, chimneys half crushed half hesitating to fall, windows guarded by rusty iron bars that time and dirt have almost eaten away, and every imaginable sign of desolation and neglect.

In such a neighbourhood, beyond Dockhead in the Borough of Southwark, stands Jacob's Island, surrounded by a muddy ditch, six or eight feet deep and fifteen or twenty wide when the tide is in, once called Mill Pond, but known in these days as Folly Ditch. It is a creek or inlet from the Thames, and can always be filled at high water by opening the sluices at the Lead Mills from which it took its old name. At such times, a stranger, looking from one of the wooden bridges thrown across it at Mill-lane, will see the inhabitants of the houses on either side lowering from their back-doors and windows, buckets, pails, domestic utensils of all kinds, in which to haul water up; and when his eye is turned from these operations to the houses themselves, his utmost astonishment will be excited by the scene before him. Crazy wooden galleries

49

common to the backs of half a dozen houses, with holes from which to look upon the slime beneath; windows, broken and patched; with poles thrust out, on which to dry the linen that is never there; rooms so small, so filthy, so confined, that the air would seem too tainted even for the dirt and squalor which they shelter; wooden chambers thrusting themselves out above the mud, and threatening to fall into it—as some have done; dirt besmeared walls and decaying foundations; every repulsive lineament of poverty, every loathsome indication of filth, rot, and garbage; all these ornament the banks of Folly Ditch.

In Jacob's Island, the warehouses are roofless and empty; the walls are crumbling down; the windows are no more; the doors are falling into the streets; the chimneys are blackened, but they yield no smoke. Thirty or forty years ago, before losses and chancery suits came upon it, it was a thriving place; but now it is a desolate island indeed. The houses have no owners; they are broken open, and entered upon by those who have the courage; and there they live, and there they die. They must have powerful motives for a secret residence, or be reduced to a destitute condition indeed, who seek a refuge in Jacob's Island.

In an upper room of one of these houses—a detached house of fair size, ruinous in other respects, but strongly defended at door and window: of which house the back commanded the ditch in manner already described—there were assembled three men, who regarding each other every now and then with looks expressive of perplexity and expectation, sat for some time in profound and gloomy silence. One of these was Toby Crackit, another Mr. Chitling, and the third a robber of fifty years, whose nose had been almost beaten in, in some old scuffle, and whose face bore a frightful scar which might probably be traced to the same occasion. This man was a returned transport, and his name was Kags.

Oliver Twist, ch. 50

If this description is to be taken literally, Jacob's Island was, without exception, the most unsalubrious locality in London. But the superlatives are not intended literally; rather they are to evoke an immediate frisson of horror appropriate to the sensational action, (the flight, pursuit, and violent death of the murderer Sikes) which the chapter is to contain. Characteristically Dickens chooses the human device of an imaginary visitor or stranger to present the scene through hypothetical eyes. Also he moves slowly from the outlying vicinity to the exterior of Jacob's Island itself, and then into the room with which he is concerned. The effect is of a slow quasi-cinematic focusing in on the presentation of the three criminals, the last of whom, as a newcomer, has to be introduced, and gives Dickens the opportunity to present a brief outline of human crime and as a climax a sinister name.

Significantly, these men themselves are only a part of the setting. Kags, indeed, has no other part in the action of the novel, and has simply been created for the effect with which he can be introduced at this point. Landscape, for Dickens, is only meaningful if it is landscape with *people*.

Although the topography of Jacob's Island is to play some part in Sikes's end, it is not for that reason that Dickens describes it so carefully. This is a typical Dickens setting, in which a careful description of place creates a strong impression of a moral or emotional environment which echoes the morality and emotions of the participants in the ensuing scene.

Structure: thematic unity

Serial composition at considerable length encouraged a loose and rambling structure. *Pickwick* was unashamedly a series of barely connected episodes. *Nicholas Nickleby* was held together by its hero's progress from genteel poverty to modest affluence. But although he was not afraid to exploit the serial form by departing from his obviously plotted course, Dickens was concerned to give his novels a more definite unity and cohesion than could be attained by reliance on the continuity of characters, authorial tone, and general emotional climate.

Little Nell's grandfather is at home in the old curiosity shop.

9

The place through which he made his way at leisure was one of those receptacles for old and curious things which seem to crouch in odd corners of this town and to hide their musty treasures from the public eye in jealousy and distrust. There were suits of mail standing like ghosts in armour here and there, fantastic carvings brought from monkish cloisters, rusty weapons of various kinds, distorted figures in china and wood and iron and ivory: tapestry and strange furniture that might have been designed in dreams. The haggard aspect of the little old man was wonderfully suited to the place; he might have groped among old churches and tombs and deserted houses and gathered all the spoils with his own hands. There was nothing in the whole collection but was in keeping with himself; nothing that looked older or more worn than he.

The Old Curiosity Shop, ch. 1

Evicted from their shop, Nell and her grandfather are travelling slowly northwards across the country. While they rest in a churchyard Nell looks at the gravestones.

10

She was looking at a humble stone which told of a young man who had died at twenty-three years old, fifty-five years ago, when she heard a faltering step approaching, and looking round saw a feeble woman bent with the weight of years, who tottered to the foot of that same grave and asked her to read the writing on the stone. The old woman thanked her when she had done, saying that she had had the words by heart for many a long, long year, but could not see them now.

'Were you his mother?' said the child.

'I was his wife, my dear.'

She the wife of a young man of three-and-twenty! Ah, true! It was fifty-five years ago.

'You wonder to hear me say that,' remarked the old woman, shaking her head. 'You're not the first. Older folk than you have wondered at the same thing before now. Yes, I was his wife. Death doesn't change us more than life, my dear.'

The Old Curiosity Shop, ch 17

Nell and her grandfather finally propose to settle at a village with an ancient church. Among those who befriend them is the sexton, who describes to Nell the existence of a deep well-shaft in the church.

II

'A dreadful place to come on in the dark!' exclaimed the child, who had followed the old man's looks and words until she seemed to stand upon its brink.

'What is it but a grave!' said the sexton. 'What else! And which of our old folks, knowing all this, thought, as the spring subsided, of their own failing strength, and lessening life? Not one!'

'Are you very old yourself?' asked the child, involuntarily.

'I shall be seventy-nine—next summer.'

'You still work when you are well?'

'Work! To be sure. You shall see my gardens hereabout. Look at the window there. I made, and have kept, that plot of ground entirely with my own hands. By this time next year I shall hardly see the sky, the boughs will have grown so thick. I have my winter work at night besides.'

He opened, as he spoke, a cupboard close to where he sat, and produced some miniature boxes, carved in a homely manner and made of old wood.

'Some gentlefolk who are fond of ancient days, and what belongs to them, 'he said, 'like to buy these keepsakes from our church and ruins. Sometimes, I make them of scraps of oak, that turn up here and there; sometimes of bits of coffins which the vaults have long preserved. See here—this is a little chest of the last kind, clasped at the edges with fragments of brass plates that had writing on 'em once, though it would be hard to read it now. I haven't many by me at this time of year, but these shelves will be full—next summer.'

The child admired and praised his work, and shortly afterwards departed; thinking as she went, how strange it was, that this old man, drawing from his pursuits, and everything around him, one stern moral, never contemplated its application to himself; and, while he dwelt upon the uncertainty of human life, seemed both in word and deed to deem himself immortal. But her musings did not stop here, for she was wise enough to think that by a good and merciful adjustment this must be human nature, and that the old sexton, with his plans for next summer, was but a type of all mankind.

Full of these meditations, she reached the church. It was easy to find the key belonging to the outer door, for each was labelled on a scrap of yellow parchment. Its very turning in the lock awoke a hollow sound, and when she entered with a faltering step, the echoes that it raised in closing made her start.

Everything in our lives, whether of good or evil, affects us most by contrast. If the peace of the simple village had moved the child more strongly, because of the dark and troubled ways that lay beyond and through which she had journeyed with such failing feet, what was the deep impression of finding herself alone in that solemn building; where the very light, coming through sunken windows, seemed old and grey, and the air, redolent of earth and mould, seemed laden with decay, purified by time of all its grosser particles, and sighing through arch and aisle, and clustered pillars, like the breath of ages gone! Here was the broken pavement, worn so long ago by pious feet, that Time, stealing on the pilgrims' steps, had trodden out their track, and left but crumbling stones. Here were the rotten beam, the sinking arch, the sapped and mouldering wall, the lowly trench of earth, the stately tomb on which no epitaph remained,—all,—marble, stone, iron, wood, and dust, one common monument of ruin. The best work and the worst the plainest and the richest, the stateliest and the least imposing—both of Heaven's work and Man's—all found one common level here, and told one common tale.

Some part of the edifice had been a baronial chapel, and here were effigies of warriors stretched upon their beds of stone with folded hands, cross-legged—those who had fought in the Holy Wars—girded with their swords, and cased in armour as they had lived. Some of these knights had their own weapons, helmets, coats of mail, hanging upon the walls hard by, and dangling from rusty hooks. Broken and dilapidated as they were, they yet retained their ancient form, and something of their ancient aspect. Thus violent deeds live after men upon the earth, and traces of war and bloodshed will survive in mournful shapes, long after those who worked the desolation are but atoms of earth themselves.

The Old Curiosity Shop, ch. 53

John Forster in his *Life of Dickens* confirmed that *The Old Curiosity Shop* was intended to be given an overall unity by similarity of places and the relevance of casually introduced characters. He wrote:

from the opening of the tale to that undesigned ending; from the image of Little Nell asleep amid the quaint grotesque figures of the old curiosity warehouse, to that other final sleep she takes among the grim forms and carvings of the old church aisle; the main purpose seems to be always present. The characters and incidents that at first appear most foreign to it, are found to have had with it a close relation.

The 'main purpose' is, of course, the journey of Nell and her grandfather, age ironically protected by childhood, to Nell's death. This subject is reinforced by the meetings with unnamed strangers, like the old woman whose young husband has died, or the unavowedly ageing sexton, who reiterate the message that age and youth are rendered uncertain in their relationship by the distorting factor of definite, but unpredictable, death.

Moreover, the strange journey through life and time is a journey through anarchic chaos: the grim chaos of mushrooming industrialism, Quilp's unco-ordinated scheming, or the decaying curiosity shop; the benign confusion of travelling showmen, wandering benefactors, and finally the pacified historical remains in the church.

The serialised novel was necessarily episodic. Dickens sought to unify the total work by relating the episodes in various ways: compare the use of weather, especially London fog and Lincolnshire rain in *Bleak House*, or the use of prisons, real and metaphorical, in *Little Dorrit*, or the use of waterways and deaths by drowning in *Our Mutual Friend*. More crudely attempted are the plots and subplots of *David Copperfield* circling around the subject of marriage, or the linkage of a variety of narratives in *Dombey and Son* through a number of notions of family. And in *Dombey and Son*, too, the parallel melodramas of Edith Dombey and Alice Brown, proud and beautiful women, sold into real or comparative prostitution by humbugging mothers, and suffering at the hands of the same villain, again give the book greater unity than might be anticipated from an enumeration of the characters whose stories are told within the novel.

Structure: introduction of extraneous or unplotted material

Although Dickens tried to unify his necessarily episodic novels to some extent, he was never afraid to exploit the freedom that serialisation gave him to introduce new material if he felt like it, to change the course of his novel if he thought this would improve sales, to alter characters drastically if this could be of use to him, and to insert fictional commentaries on questions of the day that immediately interested him.

David Copperfield and his friend Traddles are invited by their former schoolmaster Creakle, who is now a magistrate, to visit a model prison. David recognises prisoners twenty-seven and twenty-eight as Uriah Heep and Mr. Littimer. Heep, a lawyer's clerk, attempted to swindle his employer, Mr. Wickfield, and by bringing him under his power, to force his daughter Agnes Wickfield to marry him. Littimer was valet and confederate of the Byronic villain Steerforth, who seduced and abducted David's childhood sweetheart.

12

'Before I come here,' said Uriah, stealing a look at us, as

if he would have blighted the outer world to which we belonged, if he could, 'I was given to follies; but now I am sensible of my follies. There's a deal of sin outside. There's a deal of sin in mother. There's nothing but sin everywhere—except here.'

'You are quite changed?' said Mr. Creakle.

'Oh dear, yes, sir!' cried this hopeful penitent.

'You wouldn't relapse, if you were going out?' asked somebody else.

'Oh de-ar no, sir!'

'Well!' said Mr. Creakle, 'this is very gratifying. You have addressed Mr. Copperfield, Twenty Seven. Do you wish to say anything further to him?'

'You knew me a long time before I came here and was changed, Mr. Copperfield,' said Uriah, looking at me; and a more villainous look I never saw, even on his visage. 'You knew me when, in spite of my follies, I was umble among them that was proud, and meek among them that was violent—you was violent to me yourself, Mr. Copperfield. Once, you struck me a blow in the face, you know.'

General commiseration. Several indignant glances directed at me.

'But I forgive you, Mr. Copperfield,' said Uriah, making his forgiving nature the subject of a most impious and awful parallel, which I shall not record. 'I forgive everybody. It would ill become me to bear malice. I freely forgive you, and I hope you'll curb your passions in future. I hope Mr. W. will repent, and Miss W., and all of that sinful lot. You've been visited with affliction, and I hope it may do you good; but you'd better have come here. Mr. W. had better come here, and Miss W. too. The best wish I could give you, Mr. Copperfield, and give all of you gentlemen, is, that you could be took up and brought here. When I think of my past follies, and my present state, I am sure it would be best for you. I pity all who ain't brought here!'

He sneaked back into his cell, amidst a little chorus of approbation; and both Traddles and I experienced a great relief when he was locked in.

It was a characteristic feature in this repentance, that I was fain to ask what these two men had done, to be there at all. That appeared to be the last thing about which they had anything to say I addressed myself to one of the two warders, who, I suspected from certain latent indications in their faces, knew pretty well what all this stir was worth.

'Do you know,' said I, as we walked along the passage, 'what felony was Number Twenty Seven's last "folly"?'

The answer was that it was a Bank case.

'A fraud on the Bank of England?' I asked.

'Yes, sir. Fraud, forgery, and conspiracy. He and some others. He set the others on. It was a deep plot for a large sum. Sentence, transportation for life. Twentyseven was the knowingest bird of the lot, and had very nearly kept himself safe; but not quite. The Bank was just able to put salt upon his tail—and only just.'

'Do you know Twenty Eight's offence?'

'Twenty Eight,' returned my informant, speaking throughout in a low tone, and looking over his shoulder as we walked along the passage, to guard himself from being overheard, in such an unlawful reference to these Immaculates, by Creakle and the rest; 'Twenty Eight (also a transportation) got a place, and robbed a young master of a matter of two hundred and fifty pounds in money and valuables, the night before they were going abroad. I particularly recollect his case, from his being took by a dwarf.'

'A what?'

'A little woman. I have forgot her name.'

'Not Mowcher?'

'That's it! He had eluded pursuit, and was going to America in a flaxen wig and whiskers, and such a complete disguise as never you see in all your born days; when the little woman, being in Southampton, met him walking along the street—picked him out with her sharp eye in a moment—ran betwixt his legs to upset him—and held on to him like grim Death.'

'Excellent Miss Mowcher!' cried I.

'You'd have said so, if you had seen her, standing on a chair in the witness-box at the trial, as I did,' said my friend. 'He cut her face right open, and pounded her in the most brutal manner, when she took him; but she never loosed her hold till he was locked up. She held so tight to him, in fact, that the officers were obliged to take 'em both together. She gave her evidence in the gamest way, and was highly complimented by the Bench, and cheered right home to her lodgings. She said in Court that she'd have took him single-handed (on account of what she knew concerning him), if he had been Samson. And it's my belief she would!'

It was mine too, and I highly respected Miss Mowcher for it.

We had now seen all there was to see. It would have been in vain to represent to such a man as the worshipful Mr. Creakle, that Twenty Seven and Twenty Eight were perfectly consistent and unchanged; that exactly what they were then, they had always been; that the hypocritical knaves were just the subjects to make that sort of profession in such a place; that they knew its market-value at least as well as we did, in the immediate service it would do them when they were expatriated; in a word, that it was a rotten, hollow, painfully suggestive piece of business altogether. We left them to their system and themselves, and went home wondering.

'Perhaps it's a good thing, Traddles,' said I, 'to have an unsound Hobby ridden hard; for it's the sooner ridden to death.'

David Copperfield, ch. 61

The following curiosities and anomalies should be considered:

Although Mr. Micawber is imprisoned for debt, prison is in no sense a serious theme in *David Copperfield* outside this chapter.

The prison described is unquestionably burlesquing Pentonville at the time of writing (1849-50): the system, and the detail that the prisoners are awaiting transportation put this beyond doubt. But this is the *only* reference to contemporary actuality in the book, which, although appearing to cover roughly Dicken's lifespan, even omits the advent of railways, continuing coaching until the novel's end.

All that remains in this chapter from Mr. Creakle's original presentation are his name, and the fact that he admits to having been David's and Traddles' teacher. Evidently Dickens required an unsympathetic established character who could carry a promotion to the magistracy and thus invite David and Traddles to inspect the prison. Temperamentally Creakle is wrong; socially, from his role in the narrative, he was an almost inevitable choice.

Earlier in the chapter much is made of Creakle's being a Middlesex magistrate. Here the Pentonville prison system is stressed. But, notoriously, the Middlesex magistrates, who were *not* responsible for Pentonville, disapproved of its system, and used another in their own prisons. There was, however, *one* Middlesex magistrate, a Mr. Rotch, who *did* approve of Pentonville's system, and with whom Dickens had already disagreed publicly on the question of prison reform.

The whole chapter is not necessary to account for the 'final ends' of Heep and Littimer whose part in the main plot has already been played to a conclusion.

Miss Mowcher when first introduced in the book was a crony of Littimer and Steerforth. She was, however, clearly based on a real person, Mrs. Hill, who protested through her solicitors. Therefore, instead of letting her aid the villains in their plans, Dickens had once reintroduced her to state her own innocence, and now at last found a point at which to insert reported demonstrative action proving that he did not mean to defame Mrs. Hill's character.

Symbolism

People, places and things might all be introduced into Dickens' novels simply to illustrate or personify the qualities he wished to expose in some abstract concept or impersonal institution.

The narrator, Esther Summerson, is a ward of court who, in the company of two other wards in her case, Richard and Ada, has been attending proceedings in chancery. At the court Miss Flite, an eccentric disappointed litigant has invited them to come and meet her landlord, Krook, who will be interested to meet parties in their celebrated lawsuit.

13

She had stopped at a shop, over which was written KROOK, RAG AND BOTTLE WAREHOUSE. Also, in long thin letters, KROOK, DEALER IN MARINE STORES. In one part of the window was a picture of a red paper mill, at which a cart was unloading a quantity of sacks of old rags. In another, was the inscription, BONES BOUGHT. In another, LADIES' AND GENTLEMEN'S WARDROBES BOUGHT. Everything seemed to be bought, and nothing to be sold there. In all parts of the window were quantities of dirty bottles: blacking bottles, medicine bottles, ginger-beer and soda-water bottles, pickle bottles, wine bottles, ink bottles: I am reminded by mentioning the latter, that the shop had, in several little particulars, the air of being in a legal neighbourhood, and of being, as it were, a dirty hanger-on and disowned relation of the law. There were a great many ink bottles. There was a little tottering bench of shabby old volumes, outside the door, labelled 'Law Books, all at 9d.' Some of the inscriptions I have enumerated were written in law-hand, like the papers I had seen in Kenge and Carboy's office, and the letters I had so long received from the firm. Among them was one, in the same writing, having nothing to do with the business of the shop, but announcing that a respectable man aged forty-five wanted engrossing or copying to execute with neatness and despatch: Address to Nemo, care of Mr. Krook within. There were several second-hand bags, blue and red, hanging up. A little way within the shop-door, lay heaps of old crackled parchment scrolls, and discoloured and dog's-eared law-papers. I could have fancied that all the rusty keys, of which there must have been hundreds huddled together as old iron, had once belonged to doors of rooms or strong chests in lawyers' offices. The litter of rags tumbled partly into and partly out of a one-legged wooden scale, hanging without any counterpoise from a beam, might have been counsellors' bands and gowns torn up. One had only to fancy, as Richard whispered to Ada and me while we all stood looking in, that yonder bones in a corner, piled together and picked very clean, were the bones of clients, to make the picture complete.

As it was still foggy and dark, and as the shop was blinded besides by the wall of Lincoln's Inn, intercepting the light within a couple of yards, we should not have seen so much but for a lighted lantern that an old man in spectacles and a hairy cap was carrying about in the shop. Turning towards the door, he caught sight of us. He was short, cadaverous, and withered; with his head sunk sideways between his shoulders, and the breath issuing in visible smoke from his mouth, as if he were on fire within. His throat, chin, and eyebrows were so frosted with white hairs, and so gnarled with veins and puckered skin, that he looked from his breast upward, like some old root in a fall of snow.

'Hi hi!' said the old man, coming to the door. 'Have you anything to sell?'

We naturally drew back and glanced at our conductress, who had been trying to open the house-door with a key she had taken from her pocket, and to whom Richard now said that, as we had the pleasure of seeing where she lived, we would leave her, being pressed for time. But she was not to be so easily left. She became so fantastically and pressingly earnest in her entreaties that we would walk up, and see her apartment for an instant; and was so bent, in her harmless way, on leading me in, as part of the good omen she desired; that I (whatever the others might do) saw nothing for it but to comply. I suppose we were all more or less curious;—at any rate, when the old man added his persuasions to hers, and said, 'Aye, aye! Please her! It won't take a minute! Come in, come in! Come in through the shop, if t'other door's out of order! we all went in, stimulated by Richard's laughing encouragement, and relying on his protection.

'My landlord, Krook,' said the little old lady, condescending to him from her lofty station, as she presented him to us. 'He is called among the neighbours the Lord Chancellor. His shop is called the Court of Chancery. He is a very eccentric person. He is very odd. Oh, I assure you he is very odd!'

She shook her head a great many times, and tapped her forehead with her finger, to express to us that we must have the goodness to excuse him, 'For he is a little—you know!—M—!' said the old lady, with great stateliness.

Bleak House, ch. 5

Symbolism is here used for satirical purposes. Krook and his shop exist almost entirely for the sake of the parallels that may be drawn between them and the Lord Chancellor in the Court of Chancery. Krook plays little part in the plot; he is not particularly funny; he does not act as representative of a class of junk-shop keepers; the sinister nature of his house is not related to its being the *mise-en-scene* for any action more dreadful than his own death. On the other hand, consider the economy and variety of the following as satirical comments on the Lord Chancellor or the Chancery Courts:

'Everything seemed to be bought, and nothing to be sold there.'

'The litter of rags tumbled partly into and partly out of *a one-legged wooden scale, hanging without any counterpoise* from a beam, might have been *counsellor's bands and gowns* torn up.'

'As it was still foggy and dark, and as the shop *was blinded besides by the wall of Lincoln's Inn, intercepting the light* within a couple of yards . . .'

'an old man in spectacles and a hairy cap'

'For he is a little—you know!—M—!'

Serious character: mind under stress

Dickens' roots in melodrama did not leave him with a superficial taste for violent action; he rapidly developed and slowly matured a serious psychological interest in the action of the mind under unbearable stress. His murderers were not mere ruffians; even Sikes became interesting for his mental torment. Suicide and mental collapse are also common features of Dickens' writing: this is the Dickens who interested Dostoevsky.

Mr. Dombey, when a successful businessman, made a foolish second marriage to a proud woman who deserted him, eloping with his business agent. Dombey's cruel treatment of his loving daughter after the childhood death of his son has driven her away from him, and the bankruptcy of his firm has left him almost entirely friendless. Now he is alone with his memories in the upper part of his empty house.

14

He wandered through the rooms: lately so luxurious; now so bare and dismal and so changed, apparently, even in their shape and size. The press of footsteps was as thick here; and the same consideration of the suffering he had had, perplexed and terrified him. He began to fear that all this intricacy in his brain would drive him mad; and that his thoughts already lost coherence as the footprints did, and were pieced on to one another, with the same trackless involutions and varieties of indistinct shapes.

He did not so much as know in which of these rooms she had lived when she was alone. He was glad to leave them, and go wandering higher up. Abundance of associations were here, connected with his false wife, his false friend and servant, his false grounds of pride; but he put them all by now, and only recalled miserably, weakly, fondly, his two children.

Everywhere, the footsteps! They had had no respect for the old room high up, where the little bed had been; he could hardly find a clear space there, to throw himself down, on the floor, against the wall, poor broken man, and let his tears flow as they would. He had shed so many tears here, long ago, that he was less ashamed of his weakness in this place than in any other—perhaps, with that consciousness, had made excuses to himself for coming here. Here, with stooping shoulders, and his chin dropped on his breast, he had come. Here, thrown upon the bare boards, in the dead of night, he wept, alone,—a proud man, even then; who if a kind hand could have been stretched out, or a kind face could have looked in, would have risen up, and turned away, and gone down to his cell.

When the day broke he was shut up in his rooms again. He had meant to go away today, but clung to this tie in the house as the last and only thing left to him. He would go to-morrow. To-morrow came. He would go to-morrow. Every night, within the knowledge of no human creature, he came forth, and wandered through the despoiled house like a ghost. Many a morning when the day broke, his altered face, drooping behind the closed blind in his window, imperfectly transparent to the light as yet, pondered on the loss of his two children. It was one child no more. He re-united them in his thoughts, and they were never asunder. Oh, that he could have united them in his past love, and in death, and that one had not been so much worse than dead!

Strong mental agitation and disturbance was no novelty to him, even before his late sufferings. It never is, to obstinate and sullen natures; for they struggle hard to be such. Ground, long undermined, will often fall down in a moment; what was undermined here in so many ways, weakened, and crumbled, little by little, more and more, as the hand moved on the dial.

At last he began to think he need not go at all. He might yet give up what his creditors had spared him (that they had not spared him more, was his own act), and only sever the tie between him and the ruined house, by severing that other link—

It was then that his footfall was audible in the late housekeeper's room, as he walked to and fro; but not audible in its true meaning, or it would have had an appalling sound.

The world was very busy and restless about him. He became aware of that again. It was whispering and babbling. It was never quiet. This, and the intricacy and complication of the footsteps, harassed him to death. Objects began to take a bleared and russet colour in his eyes. Dombey and Son was no more—his children no more. This must be thought of, well, to-morrow.

He thought of it to-morrow; and sitting thinking in his chair, saw in the glass, from time to time, this picture:

A spectral, haggard, wasted likeness of himself, brooded and brooded over the empty fireplace. Now it lifted up its head, examining the lines and hollows in its face; now hung it down again, and brooded afresh. Now it rose and walked about; now passed into the next room, and came back with something from the dressing-table in its breast. Now, it was looking at the bottom of the door and thinking.

—Hush! what?

It was thinking that if blood were to trickle that way, and to leak out into the hall, it must be a long time going so far. It would move so stealthily and slowly, creeping on, with here a lazy little pool, and there a start, and then another little pool, that a desperately wounded man could only be discovered through its means, either dead or dying. When it had thought of this a long while, it got up again, and walked to and fro with its hands in its breast. He glanced at it occasionally, very curious to watch its motions, and he marked how wicked and murderous that hand looked.

Now it was thinking again! What was it thinking?

Whether they would tread in the blood when it crept so far, and carry it about the house among those many prints of feet, or even out into the street.

It sat down, with its eyes upon the empty fireplace, and as it lost itself in thought there shone into the room a gleam of light; a ray of sun. It was quite unmindful, and sat thinking. Suddenly it rose, with a terrible face, and that guilty hand grasping what was in its breast. Then it was arrested by a cry—a wild, loud, piercing, loving, rapturous cry— and he only saw his own reflection in the glass, and at his knees, his daughter!

Dombey and Son, ch. 59

Thus Mr. Dombey brings himself to the point of suicide, from which he is only arrested by his daughter's return.

Obviously Dickens is not completely in control of his material. There is linguistic inadequacy:

> Among those many prints of feet
> Or even out into the street.

There is uncertainty about the use to be made of the narrator's voice: who is it who is being hushed to hear what the image in the glass is thinking? Dombey has already been detached from 'himself', so that we must feel that writer and reader are being brought unnecessarily before our conciousness. 'A terrible face' is an inadequate theatrical device to suggest the intention of suicide.

But a multiplicity of fine touches remains. There is the progression of mental states: anxiety, brooding recollection, secret grief under-pinned by willed self-sufficiency, procrastinating lassitude, regret, paranoid fear of the world around, detachment from the physical self, thoughts of suicide making a strong impression on others ('Whether they would tread in the blood . . .').

There are skilful linguistic touches: '. . . imperfectly transparent to the light as yet . . .' exploits the appearance of the window at dawn to hint at Dombey's present condition as a man, not yet sufficiently cleansed of the masking pride to admit the 'light' of Florence's presence (later associated with a ray of sun). 'This must be thought of, well, tomorrow'. Is the 'well' an adverb, or an interjection indicating Dombey's fear of examining the truth about his life immediately?

Few writers could present us with so critically puzzling a passage, obvious blemishes not quite destroying a remarkable feat of sustained psychological examination. Is it really possible to say with finality whether this passage proves Dickens' understanding of the mental state he describes to be profound or vulgar?

Social criticism: emotional appeal

'Mr. Popular Sentiment,' Trollope called Dickens: Disraeli named him 'Gushy'. What they, and other similar adverse critics from that day to this, had in mind was the form of emotional appeal to social conscience which Dickens utilised, and to which Victorian audiences responded sympathetically.

Metaphorically, the fading life of Jo, a poor crossing sweeper, is described as a cart, slowly falling to pieces on a hard journey. Allan Woodcourt, a charitable doctor, has taken Jo from the slum called Tom-all-Alone's to the shooting gallery maintained by a retired trooper, where the gallery attendant, Phil Squod, nurses him. Jo, who habitually mispronounces names, refers to Mr. Snagsby, a lawstationer who furtively befriended him, and Mr. Chadband, a humbugging evangelical preacher.

15

Jo is in a sleep or in a stupor today, and Allan Woodcourt, newly arrived, stands by him, looking down upon his wasted form. After a while, he softly seats himself upon the bedside with his face towards him—just as he sat in the

72

law-writer's room—and touches his chest and heart. The cart had very nearly given up, but labours on a little more.

The trooper stands in the doorway, still and silent. Phil has stopped in a low clinking noise, with his little hammer in his hand. Mr. Woodcourt looks round with that grave professional interest and attention on his face, and, glancing significantly at the trooper, signs to Phil to carry his table out. When the little hammer is next used, there will be a speck of rust upon it.

'Well, Jo! What is the matter? Don't be frightened.'

'I thought,' says Jo, who has started, and is looking round, 'I thought I was in Tom-all-Alone's agin. Ain't there nobody here but you, Mr. Woodcot?'

'Nobody.'

'And I ain't took back to Tom-all-Alone's. Am I, sir?'

'No.' Jo closes his eyes, muttering, 'I'm wery thankful.'

After watching him closely a little while, Allan puts his mouth very near his ear, and says to him in a low, distinct voice:

'Jo! Did you ever know a prayer?'

'Never knowd nothink, sir.'

'Not so much as one short prayer?'

'No, sir. Nothink at all. Mr. Chadbands he wos a-prayin wunst at Mr. Sangsby's and I heerd him, but he sounded as if he was a-speakin to hisself, and not to me. He prayed a lot, But *I* couldn't make out nothink on it. Different times, there wos other genlmen come down Tom-all-Alone's a-prayin, but they all mostly sed as the t'other wuns prayed wrong, and all mostly sounded to be a-talkin to theirselves, or a-passin blame on the t'others, and not a-talkin to us. *We* never knowd nothink. *I* never knowd what it wos all about.'

It takes him a long time to say this; and few but an experienced and attentive listener could hear, or, hearing, understand him. After a short relapse into sleep or stupor, he makes, of a sudden, a strong effort to get out of bed.

'Stay, Jo! What now?'

'It's time for me to go to that there berryin-ground, sir,' he returns, with a wild look.

'Lie down, and tell me. What burying-ground, Jo?'

'Where they laid him as wos wery good to me, wery good to me indeed, he wos. It's time fur me to go down to that there berryin-ground, sir, and ask to be put along with him. I wants to go there and be berried. He used fur to say to me, "I am as poor as you today, Jo," he ses. I wants to tell him that I am as poor as him now, and have come there to be laid along with him.'

'By-and bye, Jo. By-and-bye.'

'Ah! P'raps they wouldn't do it if I wos to go myself. But will you promise to have me took there, sir, and laid along with him?'

'I will indeed.'

'Thank'ee, sir. Thank'ee, sir They'll have to get the key of the gate afore they can take me in, for it's allus locked. And there's a step there, as I used fur to clean with my broom.—It's turned wery dark, sir. Is there any light a-comin?'

'It is coming fast, Jo.'

Fast. The cart is shaken all to pieces, and the rugged road is very near its end.

'Jo, my poor fellow!'

'I hear you, sir, in the dark, but I'm a-gropin—a-gropin—let me catch hold of your hand.'

'Jo, can you say what I say?'

'I'll say anythink as you say, sir, fur I knows it's good.'

'OUR FATHER.'

'Our Father!—yes, that's wery good, sir.'

'WHICH ART IN HEAVEN.'

'Art in Heaven—is the light a-comin, sir?'

'It is close at hand. HALLOWED BE THY NAME!'

'Hallowed be—thy—'

The light is come upon the dark benighted way. Dead! Dead, your Majesty. Dead, my lords and gentlemen. Dead, Right Reverends and Wrong Reverends of every order. Dead, men and women, born with Heavenly com-

74

passion in your hearts. And dying thus around us every day.
Bleak House, ch. 47

The final rhetorical paragraph of this extract was famous in its day, As a challenge to the Victorian conscience it succeeded. But today we are more likely to observe the confusion of inadequately thought-out appeals to the emotions contained in the passage.

Why, for example, is the repetition of the Lord's Prayer —after the opening invocation, apparently meaningless to the dying crossing-sweeper—supposedly a better way of bringing religion to the poor than that attempted by Mr. Chadband or the 'other genlmen'? The passage never makes clear why the absence of christian knowledge is so dreadful an aggravation of the miseries of poverty as its tone and structure implies.

Of what value is the image of Jo's life as a cart falling apart on its journey along a rough road? Does it really increase our apprehension of Jo's predicament? Likewise, is the image of Jo's death as a movement from darkness into light anything more than a rather tired christian paradox, pointlessly dislocated from its exact religious import?

One cannot but observe, too, that the final peroration, technically skilful as it is (the opportunity for grim irony having returned Dickens to a surer control of his language than is exhibited elsewhere in the passage) only invites the reader to share in a comparatively comfortable moral indignation: it does not, as it speciously appears to, actually challenge the reader to re-think his own responsibilities to the poor in terms of the realities of his own life.

Social satire:
class or type representative caricature

As Dickens' art matured the one-purpose character tended to disappear. Caricatures whose sole purpose was the castigation of a social function were replaced by characters, a part of whose total function in the novel was criticism of their class or calling.

Mr. Bounderby, the leading industrialist of Coketown, makes great play with his supposedly wretched origins.

16

Mr. Bounderby being a bachelor, an elderly lady presided over his establishment, in consideration of a certain annual stipend. Mrs. Sparsit was this lady's name; and she was a prominent figure in attendance on Mr. Bounderby's car, as it rolled along in triumph with the Bully of humility inside.

For, Mrs, Sparsit had not only seen different days, but was highly connected. She had a great aunt living in these very times called Lady Scadgers. Mr. Sparsit, deceased, of whom she was the relict, had been by the mother's side what Mrs. Sparsit still called 'a Powler'. Strangers of limited information and dull apprehension were sometimes observed not to know what a Powler was, and even to appear uncertain

whether it might be a business, or a political party, or a profession of faith. The better class of minds, however, did not
need to be informed that the Powlers were an ancient stock,
who could trace themselves so exceedingly far back that
it was not surprising if they sometimes lost themselves—
which they had rather frequently done, as respected horse-
flesh, blind-hookey, Hebrew monetary transactions, and
the Insolvent Debtors' Court.

The late Mr. Sparsit, being by the mother's side a Powler,
married this lady, being by the father's side a Scadgers.
Lady Scadgers (an immensely fat old woman, with an inor-
dinate appetite for butcher's meat, and a mysterious leg
which had now refused to get out of bed for fourteen years)
contrived the marriage, at a period when Sparsit was just of
age, and chiefly noticeable for a slender body, weakly sup-
ported on two long slim props, and surmounted by no
head worth mentioning. He inherited a fair fortune from
his uncle, but owed it all before he came into it, and spent
it twice over immediately afterwards. Thus, when he died,
at twenty-four (the scene of his decease, Calais, and the
cause, brandy), he did not leave his widow, from whom he
had been separated soon after the honeymoon, in affluent
circumstances. That bereaved lady, fifteen years older than
he, fell presently at deadly feud with her only relative,
Lady Scadgers; and, partly to spite her ladyship, and
partly to maintain herself, went out at a salary. And here
she was now, in her elderly days, with the Coriolanian
style of nose and the dense black eyebrows which had
captivated Sparsit, making Mr. Bounderby's tea as he took
his breakfast.

If Bounderby had been a Conqueror, and Mrs. Sparsit
a captive Princess whom he took about as a feature in his
state-processions, he could not have made a greater flourish
with her than he habitually did. Just as it belonged to his
boastfulness to depreciate his own extraction, so it belonged
to it to exalt Mrs. Sparsit's. In the measure that he would
not allow his own youth to have been brightened by a
single favourable circumstance, he brightened Mrs. Sparsit's

juvenile career with every possible advantage, and showered waggon-loads of early roses all over that lady's path. 'And yet, sir,' he would say, 'how does it turn out after all? Why here she is at a hundred a year (I give her a hundred, which she is pleased to term handsome), keeping the house of Josiah Bounderby of Coketown!'

Nay, he made this foil of his so very widely known, that third parties took it up, and handled it on some occasions with considerable briskness. It was one of the most exasperating attributes of Bounderby, that he not only sang his own praises but stimulated other men to sing them. There was a moral infection of clap-trap in him. Strangers, modest enough elsewhere, started up at dinners in Coketown, and boasted, in quite a rampant way, of Bounderby. They made him out to be the Royal arms, the Union-Jack, Magna Charta, John Bull, Habeas Corpus, the Bill of Rights, An Englishman's house is his castle, Church and state, and God Save the Queen, all put together. And as often (and it was very often) as an orator of this kind brought into his peroration:

'Princes and lords may flourish or may fade,
A breath can make them, as a breath has made,'

it was, for certain, more or less understood among the company that he had heard of Mrs. Sparsit.

Hard Times, ch. 7

Both Bounderby and Mrs. Sparsit are characters rather than symbols: we are to be interested in and amused by them as people rather than as 'distressed gentility' or 'the self-made merchant classes'. But the jokes about each tend to refer back to the characteristics of their classes as Dickens sees them, although given appropriate individuality by such morally or socially neutral characteristics as Mrs. Sparsit's eyebrows, or Bounderby's apt, but not inevitable, orotundity of speech.

And yet, in each the degree of caricature is as marked as it might have been in the earlier wicked grotesques; the difference is that more attention is now paid to the masks of hypocrisy than to the evil beneath. Bumble and Quilp were transparent: it was hilariously funny that such manifest rogues should believe they could possibly deceive anyone into imagining them honest. The palpable fact that one would have expected them to be arrested on sight gave their villainy an innocent quality. Bounderby and Mrs. Sparsit only give themselves away by the strained and overdone quality of their poses. Where Bumble's pretence of charity or political philosophy was obviously at odds with his character, we only sense the gap between mask and reality in the later figures because Mrs. Sparsit's gentility is *too* perfectly meaningless to be true; Bounderby is *too* perfect a rags-to-riches figure from Samuel Smiles.

Serious dialogue: restrained

In maturity, Dickens achieved an increasingly sure control over his treatment of serious and dramatic themes and moments, and was able to abandon many of the melodramatic techniques on which he had earlier relied.

Pip, the narrator, is apprenticed to Joe the blacksmith. But he has been exposed to genteel life when, as a child, he was employed to play with eccentric Miss Havisham's ward Estella. Now he voices his discontent to Biddy Wopsle, who once assisted at the dame school he attended.

17

When we came to the river-side and sat down on the bank, with the water rippling at our feet, making it all more quiet than it would have been without that sound, I resolved that it was a good time and place for the admission of Biddy into my inner confidence.

'Biddy,' said I, after binding her to secrecy, 'I want to be a gentleman.'

'Oh, I wouldn't if I was you!' she returned. 'I don't think it would answer.'

'Biddy,' said I with some severity, 'I have particular reasons for wanting to be a gentleman.'

'You know best, Pip; but don't you think you are happier as you are?'

'Biddy,' I exclaimed, impatiently, 'I am not at all happy as I am. I am disgusted with my calling and with my life. I have never taken to either since I was bound. Don't be absurd.'

'Was I absurd?' said Biddy, quietly raising her eyebrows; 'I am sorry for that; I didn't mean to be. I only want you to do well and be comfortable.'

'Well, then, understand once for all that I never shall or can be comfortable—or anything but miserable—there, Biddy!—unless I can lead a very different sort of life from the life I lead now.'

'That's a pity!' said Biddy, shaking her head with a sorrowful air.

Now, I too had so often thought it a pity, that, in the singular kind of quarrel with myself which I was always carrying on, I was half inclined to shed tears of vexation and distress when Biddy gave utterance to her sentiment and my own. I told her she was right, and I knew it was much to be regretted, but still it was not to be helped.

'If I could have settled down,' I said to Biddy, plucking up the short grass within reach, much as I had once upon a time pulled my feelings out of my hair and kicked them into the brewery wall: 'if I could have settled down and been but half as fond of the forge as I was when I was little, I know it would have been much better for me. You and I and Joe would have wanted nothing then, and Joe and I would perhaps have gone partners when I was out of my time, and I might even have grown up to keep company with you, and we might have sat on this very bank on a fine Sunday, quite different people. I should have been good enough for *you*: shouldn't I, Biddy?'

Biddy sighed as she looked at the ships sailing on, and returned for answer, 'Yes; I am not over-particular.' It scarcely sounded flattering, but I knew she meant well.

'Instead of that,' said I, plucking up more grass and

81

chewing a blade or two, 'see how I am going on. Dissatisfied and uncomfortable, and—what would it signify to me, being coarse and common, if nobody had told me so!'

Biddy turned her face suddenly towards mine, and looked far more attentively at me than she had looked at the sailing ships.

'It was neither a very true nor a very polite thing to say,' she remarked, directing her eyes to the ships again. 'Who said it?'

I was disconcerted, for I had broken away without quite seeing where I was going to. It was not to be shuffled off, now, however, and I answered, 'The beautiful young lady at Miss Havisham's, and she's more beautiful than anybody ever was, and I admire her dreadfully, and I want to be a gentleman on her account.' Having made this lunatic confession, I began to throw my torn-up grass into the river, as if I had some thoughts of following it.

'Do you want to be a gentleman, to spite her or to gain her over?' Biddy quietly asked me, after a pause.

'I don't know,' I moodily answered.

'Because, if it is to spite her,' Biddy pursued, 'I should think—but you know best—that might be better and more independently done by caring nothing for her words. And if it is to gain her over, I should think—but you know best—she was not worth gaining over.'

Exactly what I myself had thought, many times. Exactly what was perfectly manifest to me at the moment. But how could I, a poor dazed village lad, avoid that wonderful inconsistency into which the best and wisest of men fall every day?

'It may all be quite true,' said I to Biddy, 'but I admire her dreadfully.'

In short, I turned over on my face when I came to that, and got a good grasp on my hair, on each side of my head, and wrenched it well. All the while knowing the madness of my heart to be so very mad and misplaced, that I was quite conscious it would have served my face right, if I had lifted it up by the hair, and knocked it against the pebbles as a punishment for belonging to such an idiot.

Biddy was the wisest of girls, and she tried to reason no more with me. She put her hand, which was a comfortable hand though roughened by work, upon my hands, one after another, and gently took them out of my hair. Then she softly patted my shoulder in a soothing way, while with my face upon my sleeve I cried a little—exactly as I had done in the brewery yard—and felt vaguely convinced that I was much ill-used by somebody, or by everybody; I can't say which.

'I am glad of one thing,' said Biddy, 'and that is, that you have felt you could give me your confidence, Pip. And I am glad of another thing, and that is, that of course you know you may depend upon my keeping it and always so far deserving it. If your first teacher (dear! such a poor one, and so much in need of being taught herself!) had been your teacher at the present time, she thinks she knows what lesson she would set. But it would be a hard one to learn, and you have got beyond her, and it's of no use now.' So, with a quiet sigh for me, Biddy rose from the bank, and said, with a fresh and pleasant change of voice, 'Shall we walk a little further, or go home?'

'Biddy,' I cried, getting up, putting my arm around her neck, and giving her a kiss, 'I shall always tell you everything.'

'Till you're a gentleman,' said Biddy.

'You know I never shall be, so that's always. Not that I have any reason to tell you anything, for you know everything I know—as I told you at home the other night.'

'Ah!' said Biddy, quite in a whisper, as she looked away at the ships. And then repeated, with her former pleasant change, 'Shall we walk a little further, or go home?'

I said to Biddy we would walk a little further, and we did so, and the summer afternoon toned down into the summer evening, and it was very beautiful.

Great Expectations, ch. 17

With tact and economy Dickens presents a complex emotional situation. Pip's immature lack of control over his emotions is presented through his diction, his actions, and the fact that he 'cries', 'exclaims', and speaks severely or moodily, while Biddy 'says', and moves, as a rule, slowly and quietly.

Biddy's unrequited love for Pip is superbly registered in quiet notes: her true observation that she wishes Pip to do well and be comfortable, her sigh when Pip carelessly disparages her, her sudden movement when she hears of an insult to Pip, and her loss of countenance at Pip's insensitivity in observing but not appreciating her grasp of his thought.

The ironies and misunderstandings occasioned by Pip's callowness give the scene an uncomfortable and embarrassing quality, which is softly heightened by the flowing concluding sentence, which ironically frames the whole as though it had been an idyllic love passage.

Behind the whole, carefully controlling the scene, is the assumed voice of the mature Pip, presenting his former weakness and folly with calm detachment.

Insularity

Although by middle age Dickens was a much-travelled man and a fine linguist, he remained narrowly English in his attitude to foreign countries and customs: typically he is parochially suspicious of foreigners, but not jingoistically or boastfully patriotic.

Mr. Dorrit, a former prisoner in the Marshalsea, has been distressed by a visit from John Chivery, his former gaoler's son, who gave him a bundle of cigars. Mr. Dorrit hopes that by presenting these to the Courier who is guiding him on a continental tour he may exorcise the past and enjoy the prospect of a happily respectable marriage—his castle in the air.

18

Not a fortified town that they passed in all their journey was as strong, not a Cathedral summit was as high, as Mr. Dorrit's castle. Neither the Saone nor the Rhone sped with the swiftness of that peerless building; nor was the Mediterranean deeper than its foundations; nor were the distant landscapes on the Cornice road, nor the hills and bay of Genoa the Superb, more beautiful. Mr. Dorrit and his matchless castle were disembarked among the dirty white houses and dirtier felons of Civita Vecchia, and thence scrambled on to Rome as they could, through the filth that festered on the way.

The sun had gone down full four hours, and it was later than most travellers would like it to be for finding themselves outside the walls of Rome, when Mr. Dorrit's carriage, still on its last wearisome stage, rattled over the solitary Campagna. The savage herdsmen and the fierce-looking peasants, who had chequered the way while the light lasted, had all gone down with the sun, and left the wilderness blank. At some turns of the road, a pale flare on the horizon, like an exhalation from the ruin-sown land, showed that the city was yet far off; but, this poor relief was rare and short-lived. The carriage dipped down again into a hollow of the black dry sea and for a long time there was nothing visible save its petrified swell and the gloomy sky.

Mr. Dorrit, though he had his castle-building to engage his mind, could not be quite easy in that desolate place. He was far more curious, in every swerve of the carriage, and every cry of the postilions than he had been since he quitted London. The valet on the box evidently quaked. The Courier in the rumble was not altogether comfortable in his mind. As often as Mr. Dorrit let down the glass and looked back at him (which was very often), he saw him smoking John Chivery out, it is true, but still generally standing up the while and looking about him, like a man who had his suspicions, and kept upon his guard. Then would Mr. Dorrit, pulling up the glass again, reflect that those postilions were cut-throat looking fellows, and that he would have done better to have slept at Civita Vecchia, and have started betimes in the morning. But, for all this, he worked at his castle in the intervals.

And now, fragments of ruinous enclosure, yawning window-gap and crazy wall, deserted houses, leaking wells, broken water-tanks, spectral cypress-trees, patches of

tangled vine, and the changing of the track to a long,
irregular, disordered lane, where everything was crumbling away, from the unsightly buildings to the jolting
road—now, these objects showed that they were nearing
Rome. And now, a sudden twist and stoppage of the carriage inspired Mr. Dorrit with the mistrust that the brigand
moment was come for twisting him into a ditch and robbing
him; until, letting down the glass again and looking out,
he perceived himself assailed by nothing worse than a
funeral procession, which came mechanically chaunting
by, with an indistinct show of dirty vestments, lurid
torches, swinging censers, and a great cross borne before
a priest. He was an ugly priest by torch-light; of a lowering aspect, with an overhanging brow; and as his eyes met
those of Mr. Dorrit, looking bareheaded out of the carriage,
his lips, moving as they chaunted, seemed to threaten that
important traveller; likewise the action of his hand, which
was in fact his manner of returning the traveller's saluta-
tion, seemed to come in aid of that menace. So thought
Mr. Dorrit, made fanciful by the weariness of building and
travelling, as the priest drifted past him, and the procession
straggled away, taking its dead along with it. Upon their
so-different way went Mr. Dorrit's company too; and
soon, with their coach-load of luxuries from the two great
capitals of Europe, they were (like the Goths reversed)
beating at the gates of Rome.

Little Dorrit, chs. 54-55

The maturity of Dickens' art is well exhibited in the
skill with which Mr. Dorrit's castle-in-the-air is inter-
woven with the real castles and ramshackle landscape
through which he passes, and the contrasting of his
tourist vulgarity of display with the Italian vulgarity of
decay.

But the limitation of Dickens' outlook may be seen from
the 'savagery' of the herdsmen—(British labourers might
be fierce, but a suggestion of the primitive would not be

87

applied to them by Dickens)—and the absolutely characteristic suspicion of any manifestation of Roman Catholi-
cism, evidence of a Protestantism more nationalistic than
religious.

Prose technique

It should by now be clear that Dickens was capable of adapting his style to his purpose, and that, in fact, one finds in his novels a variety of styles, often judged to be good or bad much as their subject appears to be good or bad. It should not, then, be forgotten that this characteristic is really evidence of a superlative mastery over language which may best be observed when it is not being used for narrative, humour, or humane appeal, but simply to hold the reader's attention by its own virtuosity.

The opening of *A Tale of Two Cities* describes the period in which the book is set.

19

It was the best of times, it was the worst of times, it was the age of wisdom, it was the age of foolishness, it was the epoch of belief, it was the epoch of incredulity, it was the season of Light, it was the season of Darkness, it was the spring of hope, it was the winter of despair, we had everything before us, we had nothing before us, we were all going direct to Heaven, we were all going direct the other way—in short, the period was so far like the present period, that some of its noisiest authorities insisted on its being received, for good or evil, in the superlative degree of comparison only.

There were a king with a large jaw and a queen with a plain face, on the throne of England; there were a king with a large jaw and a queen with a fair face, on the throne of France. In both countries it was clearer than crystal to the lords of the State preserves of loaves and fishes, that things in general were settled for ever.

It was the year of Our Lord one thousand seven hundred and seventy-five. Spiritual revelations were conceded to England at that favoured period, as at this. Mrs. South-cott had recently attained her five-and-twentieth birthday, of whom a prophetic private in the Life Guards had heralded the sublime appearance by announcing that arrangements were made for the swallowing up of London and Westminster. Even the Cock-lane ghost had been laid only a round dozen of years, after rapping out its messages, as the spirits of this very year last past (supernaturally deficient in originality) rapped out theirs. Mere messages in the earthly order of events had lately come to the English Crown and People, from a congress of British subjects in America: which, strange to relate, have proved more important to the human race than any communications yet received through any of the chickens of the Cock-Lane brood.

France, less favoured on the whole as to matters spiritual than her sister of the shield and trident, rolled with exceeding smoothness down hill, making paper money and spending it. Under the guidance of her Christian pastors, she entertained herself, besides, with such humane achievements as sentencing a youth to have his hands cut off, his tongue torn out with pincers, and his body burned alive, because he had not kneeled down in the rain to do honour to a dirty procession of monks which passed within his view, at a distance of some fifty or sixty yards. It is likely enough that, rooted in the woods of France and Norway, there were growing trees, when

90

that sufferer was put to death, already marked by the Woodman, Fate, to come down and be sawn into boards, to make a certain movable framework with a sack and a knife in it, terrible in history. It is likely enough that in the rough outhouses of some tillers of the heavy lands adjacent to Paris, there were sheltered from the weather that very day, rude carts, bespattered with rustic mire, snuffed about by pigs, and roosted in by poultry, which the Farmer, Death, had already set apart to be his tumbrils of the Revolution. But that Woodman and that Farmer, though they work unceasingly, work silently, and no one heard them as they went about with muffled tread: the rather, forasmuch as to entertain any suspicion that they were awake was to be atheistical and traitorous.

In England there was scarcely an amount of order and protection to justify much national boasting. Daring burglaries by armed men, and highway robberies, took place in the capital itself every night; families were publicly cautioned not to go out of town without removing their furniture to upholsterers' warehouses for security; the highwayman in the dark was a City tradesman in the light, and, being recognised and challenged by his fellow-tradesman whom he stopped in his character of 'the Captain,' gallantly shot him through the head and rode away; the mail was waylaid by seven robbers, and the guard shot three dead, and then got shot dead himself by the other four, 'in consequence of the failure of his ammunition:' after which the mail was robbed in peace; that magnificent potentate, the Lord Mayor of London, was made to stand and deliver on Turnham Green, by one highwayman, who despoiled the illustrious creature in sight of all his retinue; prisoners in London gaols fought battles with their turnkeys, and the majesty of the law fired blunderbusses in among them, loaded with rounds of shot and ball; thieves snipped off diamond crosses from the necks of noble lords at Court drawing-rooms; musketeers went into St. Giles's, to search for contraband goods, and the mob fired on the musketeers, and the musketeers fired on the mob, and nobody thought any of these occurrences much out of the common way. In the midst of them, the hangman, ever busy and ever worse than useless, was in constant requisition; now, stringing up long rows of miscellaneous criminals; now, hanging a housebreaker on Saturday who had been taken on Tuesday; now, burning people in the hand at Newgate by the dozen, and now burning pamphlets at the door of Westminster Hall; to-day, taking the life of an atrocious murderer, and to-morrow of a wretched pilferer who had robbed a farmer's boy of sixpence.

All these things, and a thousand like them, came to pass in and close upon the dear old year one thousand seven hundred and seventy-five. Environed by them, while the Woodman and the Farmer worked unheeded, those two of the large jaws, and those other two of the plain and the fair faces, trod with stir enough, and carried their divine rights with a high hand. Thus did the year one thousand seven hundred and seventy-five conduct their Greatnesses, and myriads of small creatures—the creatures of this chronicle among the rest—along the roads that lay before them.

A Tale of Two Cities, ch. 1

In this magnificent opening Dickens seeks to hold the reader's attention by reducing chaos to disguised order. His opening sentence—really a series of unpunctuated sentences—gives the appearance of chaos by its speedy contradictions; actually it is almost blatantly ordered in that the pairs of opposites make every second clause completely predictable.

Parallel pairs are extended in the second paragraph to present the comparison between the two countries. In the third paragraph Dickens sets up a slightly supercilious ironical tone of moral condemnation which is to be used throughout the book with reference to England. The fourth paragraph provides the parallel grimly Carlylean irony which is to be used for France, and predicts the subject of the book. The fifth paragraph shows that England is certainly not going to be held up as a perfect moral exemplar to France; indicates the theme of lawlessness which is to be peculiarly English in the book, and returns to the suggestion of anarchy which the opening sentence appeared to indicate. And the last paragraph leads back to the notion of specific people directing their individual lives through this historical climate, and so prepares us for the opening of the action.

Plain narrative prose

Even without technical fireworks, Dickens' prose came to be an instrument he could use confidently to introduce or sustain effects not necessarily apparent in the matter of his writing. This becomes obvious in a comparison of the original with the revised ending of *Great Expectations*, when 300 words which concluded the predetermined plot had to be expanded to 1000 to meet Bulwer Lytton's suggestion that the book be given a happy ending. No new incident was introduced, but a nostalgic setting and languid conversation cunningly slid the story away from a predictable dip into tragedy.

Pip, the narrator, long entertained a belief that he was destined to marry Estella, the beautiful ward of Miss Havisham, who had lived in the old house adjoining the brewery. In fact, Estella was being deliberately educated to hate and despise men, and in spite of her warnings to Pip that he was not exempt from her inability to love, he nursed a hopeless passion for her, and was heartbroken when she contemptuously married his worthless rival Bentley Drummle. Eleven years after these events, Pip, still a bachelor, has made his fortune abroad, and is revisiting his English friends Joe and Biddy, whose little son is named after him, when he thinks again of Estella.

20

I had heard of her as leading a most unhappy life, and as being separated from her husband who had used her with great cruelty, and who had become quite renowned as a compound of pride, brutality and meanness. I had heard of the death of her husband (from an accident consequent on ill-treating a horse), and of her being married again to a Shropshire doctor, who, against his interest, had once very manfully interposed, on an occasion when he was in professional attendance on Mr. Drummle, and had witnessed some outrageous treatment of her. I had heard that the Shropshire doctor was not rich, and that they lived on her own personal fortune. I was in England again—in London, and walking along Piccadilly with little Pip—when a servant came running after me to ask would I step back to a lady in a carriage who wished to speak to me. It was a little pony carriage, which the lady was driving; and the lady and I looked sadly enough on one another. 'I am greatly changed, I know; but I thought you would like to shake hands with Estella too, Pip. Lift up that pretty child and let me kiss it!' (She supposed the child, I think, to be my child.) I was very glad afterwards to have had the interview; for, in her face, and in her voice, and in her touch, she gave me the assurance, that suffering had been stronger than Miss Havisham's teaching, and had given her a heart to understand what my heart used to be.

Great Expectations, cancelled conclusion to ch. 58

21

I had heard of her as leading a most unhappy life, and as being separated from her husband, who had used her with great cruelty, and who had become quite renowned as a compound of pride, avarice, brutality, and meanness. And I had heard of the death of her husband, from an accident consequent on his ill-treatment of a horse. This release had befallen her two years before; for anything I knew, she was married again.

The early dinner-hour at Joe's left me abundance of time, without hurrying my talk with Biddy, to walk over to the old spot before dark. But, what with loitering on the way, to look at old objects and to think of old times, the day had quite declined when I came to the place.

There was no house now, no brewery, no building whatever left, but the wall of the old garden. The cleared space had been enclosed with a rough fence, and looking over it, I saw that some of the old ivy had struck root anew, and was growing green on low quiet mounds of ruin. A gate in the fence standing ajar, I pushed it open and went in.

A cold silvery mist had veiled the afternoon, and the moon was not yet up to scatter it. But the stars were shining beyond the mist, and the moon was coming, and the evening was not dark. I could trace out where every part of the old house had been, and where the brewery had been, and where the gates, and where the casks. I had done so, and was looking along the desolate garden-walk, when I beheld a solitary figure in it.

The figure showed itself aware of me as I advanced. It had been moving towards me, but it stood still. As I drew nearer, I saw it to be the figure of a woman. As I drew nearer yet, it was about to turn away, when it stopped, and let me come up with it. Then, it faltered as if much surprised, and uttered my name, and I cried out:

'Estella!'

'I am greatly changed. I wonder you know me.'

The freshness of her beauty was indeed gone, but its indescribable majesty and its indescribable charm remained. Those attractions in it I had seen before; what I had never seen before was the saddened softened light of the once proud eyes; what I had never felt before was the friendly touch of the once insensible hand.

We sat down on a bench that was near, and I said, 'After

so many years, it is strange that we should thus meet again, Estella, here where our first meeting was! Do you often come back?'

'I have never been here since.'

'Nor I.'

The moon began to rise, and I thought of the placid look at the white ceiling, which had passed away. The moon began to rise, and I thought of the pressure on my hand when I had spoken the last words he had heard on earth.

Estella was the next to break the silence that ensued between us.

'I have very often hoped and intended to come back, but have been prevented by many circumstances. Poor, poor old place!'

The silvery mist was touched with the first rays of the moonlight, and the same rays touched the tears that dropped from her eyes. Not knowing that I saw them, and setting herself to get the better of them, she said quietly:

'Were you wondering, as you walked along, how it came to be left in this condition?'

'Yes, Estella.'

'The ground belongs to me. It is the only possession I have not relinquished. Everything else has gone from me, little by little, but I have kept this. It was the subject of the only determined resistance I made in all the wretched years.'

'Is it to be built on?'

'At last it is. I came here to take leave of it before its change. And you,' she said, in a voice of touching interest to a wanderer, 'you live abroad still.'

'Still.'

'And do well, I am sure?'

'I work pretty hard for a sufficient living, and there-fore— Yes, I do well!'

'I have often thought of you,' said Estella.

'Have you?'

'Of late, very often. There was a long hard time when

I kept far from me the remembrance of what I had
thrown away when I was quite ignorant of its worth.
But, since my duty has not been incompatible with the
admission of that remembrance, I have given it a place in
my heart.'

'You have always held your place in *my* heart,' I answered.

And we were silent again until she spoke.

'I little thought,' said Estella, 'that I should take leave
of you in taking leave of this spot. I am very glad to do
so.'

'Glad to part again, Estella? To me parting is a painful
thing. To me, the remembrance of our last parting has been
ever mournful and painful.'

'But you said to me,' returned Estella, very earnestly,
' "God bless you, God forgive you!" And if you could
say that to me then, you will not hesitate to say that to
me now—now, when suffering has been stronger than all
other teaching, and has taught me to understand what your
heart used to be. I have been bent and broken, but—I hope
—into a better shape. Be as considerate and good to me
as you were, and tell me we are friends.'

'We are friends,' said I, rising and bending over her as
she rose from the bench.

'And will continue friends apart,' said Estella.

I took her hand in mine, and we went out of the ruined
place; and, as the morning mists had risen long ago when
I first left the forge, so, the evening mists were rising
now, and in all the broad expanse of tranquil light they
showed to me, I saw no shadow of another parting from
her.

Great Expectations, ch. 59

In the second passage, Dickens is clearly at pains to
impress us with the moving nature of the uncertainly
happy ending he offers. There are poetic words: moon,
ruins, mist. And there is, in the paragraph rhetorically
repeating the phrase, 'The moon began to rise,' a powerful
reference back to the death of Estella's convict father,

whose relationship with Pip was one of the most important and successful parts of the main novel.

Nonetheless, the first passage is, in context, as effective as the second. Given a carefully plotted and convincingly attained situation, Dickens can employ a flat, almost awkward narrative prose, to set off light touches in which delicate, but poignant, emotional points are made. The first version's opening succession of 'I had heard' sentences is as clumsy, and suggestive of an amateur raconteur, as the repetitions of the revised version are deft, and suggestive of the professional *romancier*. But the sudden understatement of, 'the lady and I looked sadly enough on one another,' justifies the clumsiness. The notion that Pip and Estella have become emotional flotsam would be difficult for Pip to state without sentimentality: even an understatement might have looked like a manfully posed stiff upper lip. Therefore, a touch of drab writing *before* the wry observation highlights it, without rendering it self-conscious. Note, then, the charged implication of the one word 'too' in Estella's speech. After this, the rhetorical succession, 'in her face, and in her voice, and in her touch,' and the poetic comparison of hearts comprise a sentence which is not so highly written as to overbalance the passage, but is in no way a feeble ending to the story of Pip's love for Estella. The final phrases take an added force from the dull preceding prose, which suggests the drab everyday life, in which a flawed love affair like that of Pip and Estella is still a colourful incident.

Serious villains

Unsurprisingly, Dickens' increasingly sober view of life in his later works forced him to create villains who were no longer mere stereotypes, or black figures from popular melodrama. Although the black-and-white moral judgements remain, the view of life is harsher, for all its restraint, when murderers may be seemingly ordinary people.

Bradley Headstone, a schoolmaster, has taken Charley Hexam, the son of a disreputable Thames-side scavenger, from the 'jumble', a squalid slum school, into his own school. Subsequently Headstone is to fall in love with Hexam's sister, and attempt to murder her aristocratic lover, having first disguised himself as a waterside ruffian.

22

Even in this temple of good intentions, an exceptionally sharp boy exceptionally determined to learn, could learn something, and, having learned it, could impart it much better than the teachers; as being more knowing than they, and not at the disadvantage in which they stood towards the shrewder pupils. In this way it had come about that Charley Hexam had risen in the jumble, taught in the jumble, and been received from the jumble into a better school.

'So you want to go and see your sister, Hexam?'

'If you please, Mr. Headstone.'

'I have half a mind to go with you. Where does your sister live?'

'Why, she is not settled yet, Mr. Headstone. I'd rather you didn't see her till she's settled, if it was all the same to you.'

'Look here, Hexam.' Mr. Bradley Headstone, highly certificated stipendiary schoolmaster, drew his right forefinger through one of the buttonholes of the boy's coat, and looked at it attentively. 'I hope your sister may be good company for you?'

'Why do you doubt it, Mr. Headstone?'

'I did not say I doubted it.'

'No sir; you didn't say so.'

Bradley Headstone looked at his finger again, took it out of the buttonhole and looked at it closer, bit the side of it and looked at it again.

'You see, Hexam, you will be one of us. In good time you are sure to pass a creditable examination and become one of us. Then the question is—'

The boy waited so long for the question, while the schoolmaster looked at a new side of his finger, and bit it, and looked at it again, that at length the boy repeated:

'The question is, sir—?'

'Whether you had not better leave well alone.'

'Is it well to leave my sister alone, Mr. Headstone?'

'I do not say so, because I do not know. I put it to you, I ask you to think of it. I want you to consider. You know how well you are doing here.'

'After all, she got me here,' said the boy with a struggle.

'Perceiving the necessity of it,' acquiesced the schoolmaster, 'and making up her mind fully to the separation. Yes.'

The boy, with a return of that former reluctance or struggle or whatever it was, seemed to debate with himself. At length he said, raising his eyes to the master's face :

'I wish you'd come with me and see her, Mr. Headstone, though she is not settled. I wish you'd come with me, and take her in the rough, and judge for yourself.'

'You are sure you would not like,' asked the schoolmaster, 'to prepare her?'

'My sister Lizzie,' said the boy, proudly, 'wants no preparing, Mr. Headstone. What she is, she is, and shows herself to be. There's no pretending about my sister.'

His confidence in her sat more easily upon him than the indecision with which he had twice contended. It was his better nature to be true to her, if it were his worse nature to be wholly selfish. And as yet the better nature had the stronger hold.

'Well, I can spare the evening,' said the schoolmaster. 'I am ready to walk with you.'

'Thank you, Mr. Headstone. And I am ready to go.'

Bradley Headstone, in his decent black coat and waistcoat, and decent white shirt, and decent black formal tie, and decent pantaloons of pepper and salt, with his decent silver watch in his pocket and its decent hair-guard round his neck, looked a thoroughly decent young man of six-and-twenty. He was never seen in any other dress, and yet there was a certain stiffness in his manner of wearing this, as if there were a want of adaptation between him and it, recalling some mechanics in their holiday clothes. He had acquired mechanically a great store of teacher's knowledge. He could do mental arithmetic mechanically, sing at sight mechanically, blow various wind instruments mechanically, even play the great church organ mechanically. From his early childhood up, his mind had been a place of mechanical stowage. The arrangement of his wholesale warehouse, so that it might be always ready to meet the demands of retail dealers—history here, geography there, astronomy to the right, political economy to the left—natural history, the physical sciences, figures, music, the lower mathematics, and what not, all in their several places—this care had imparted to his countenance a look of care; while the habit of questioning and being questioned had given him a suspicious manner, or a manner that would be better described as one of lying in wait. There was a kind of settled trouble in the face. It was the face belonging to a naturally slow or inattentive intellect that had toiled hard to get what it had won, and that had to hold it now that it was gotten. He always seemed to be uneasy lest anything should be missing from his mental warehouse, and taking stock to assure himself.

Suppression of so much to make room for so much, had given him a constrained manner, over and above. Yet there was enough of what was animal, and of what was fiery (though smouldering), still visible in him, to suggest that if young Bradley Headstone, when a pauper lad, had chanced to be told off for the sea, he would not have been the last man in a ship's crew. Regarding that origin of his, he was proud, moody, and sullen, desiring it to be forgotten. And few people knew of it.

In some visits to the Jumble his attention had been drawn to this boy Hexam. An undeniable boy for a pupil-teacher; an undeniable boy to do credit to the master who should bring him on. Combined with this consideration there may have been some thought of the pauper lad now never to be mentioned. Be that how it might, he had with pains gradually worked the boy into his own school, and procured him some offices to discharge there, which were repaid with food and lodging. Such were the circumstances that had brought together Bradley Headstone and young Charley Hexam that autumn evening.

Our Mutual Friend, Bk. II, ch. 1

At this stage of his career, Bradley Headstone is not apparently an unredeemable villain. Unlike Quilp, Bumble, Bounderby or Mrs. Sparsit, who never show any signs of unselfishness, Headstone does perhaps show the capacity

103

to feel for others by comparing their experience with his own as a pauper lad.

His conversation with Charley is totally unfunny, and in no way openly villainous. An inhuman coldness is suggested in his attitude to Charley's family ties, but social unease is shown to cause this. There is no vigorous acceptance of malevolence.

Headstone's description is clearly by the physical observer of Dickens' earlier work. The catalogue of relevant clothes, repeated key-words ('decent' and 'mechanical') and the far-fetched image of the mind as a warehouse in a commercial economy, are conventionally (and brilliantly) Dickensian. But the total effect is strangely harsh and muted. 'Decent' comes to sound like a curse; 'mechanical' is introduced with the marvellously subtle reference to artisan 'mechanics' which contrasts holidaying humanity with the coldness of Headstone. The elaborate image of the warehouse seems more to be surprisingly accurate than comically curious.

The fiery spirit which is ultimately to determine the extreme course of Headstone's corruption is introduced last and briefly; it is, after all, repressed, and Dickens' psychological observation is now so acute and sure that he can clearly note repression as more dangerous than wildness.

Social satire:
caricature of class or institution

It was not always necessary for Dickens to reduce a class or profession to one representative, or one symbolic figure. If necessary he could sketch a quick caricature of an entire class or institution in action.

The great establishment family of the Tite Barnacles are gathered for a society wedding.

23

There was Mr. Tite Barnacle, from the Circumlocution Office, and Mews Street, Grosvenor Square, with the expensive Mrs. Tite Barnacle *nee* Stiltstalking, who made the Quarter Days so long in coming, and the three expensive Miss Tite Barnacles, double-loaded with accomplishments and ready to go off, and yet not going off with the sharpness of Flash and bang that might have been expected, but rather hanging fire. There was Barnacle Junior, also from the Circumlocution Office, leaving the Tonnage of the country, which he was somehow supposed to take under his protection, to look after itself, and, sooth to say, not at all impairing the efficiency of its protection by leaving it alone. There was the engaging Young Barnacle, deriving from the sprightly side of the family, also from the Circumlocution Office, gaily and agreeably helping the occasion along, and treating it, in his sparkling way, as one of the official forms and fees of the Church Department of How not to do it. There were three other Young Barnacles, from three other offices, insipid to all the senses, and terribly in want of seasoning, doing the marriage as they would have 'done' the Nile, Old Rome, the new singer, or Jerusalem.

But there was greater game than this. There was Lord Decimus Tite Barnacle himself, in the odour of Circumlocution—with the very smell of Despatch-Boxes upon him. Yes, there was Lord Decimus Tite Barnacle, who had risen to official heights on the wings of one indignant idea, and that was, My Lords, that I am yet to be told that it behoves a Minister of this free country to set bounds to the philanthropy, to cramp the charity, to fetter the public spirit, to contract the enterprise, to damp the independent self-reliance, of its people. That was, in other words, that this great statesman was always yet to be told that it behoved the Pilot of the ship to do anything but prosper in the private loaf and fish trade ashore, the crew being able, by dint of hard pumping, to keep the ship above water without him. On this sublime discovery, in the great art of How not to do it, Lord Decimus had long sustained the highest glory of the Barnacle family; and let any ill-advised member of either House but try How to do it, by bringing in a Bill to do it, that Bill was as good as dead and buried when Lord Decimus Tite Barnacle rose up in his place, and solemnly said, soaring into indignant majesty as the Circumlocution cheering soared around him, that he was yet to be told, My Lords, that it behoved him as the Minister of this free country, to set bounds to the philanthropy, to cramp the charity, to fetter the public spirit, to contract the enterprise, to damp the independent self-reliance, of its people. The discovery of this Behoving Machine was the discovery of the political perpetual motion. It never wore out, though it was always going round and round in all the state Departments.

And there, with his noble friend and relative Lord Decimus, was William Barnacle, who had made the ever-famous coalition with Tudor Stiltstalking, and who always kept ready his own particular recipe for How not to do it; sometimes tapping the Speaker, and drawing it fresh out of him, with a 'First, I will beg you, sir, to inform the House what Precedent we have for the course into which the honourable gentleman would precipitate us;' sometimes telling the honourable gentleman that he (William Barnacle) would search for a Precedent; and oftentimes crushing the honourable gentleman flat on the spot, by telling him there was no Precedent. But, Precedent and Precipitate were, under all circumstances, the well-matched pair of battle-horses of this able Circumlocutionist. No matter that the unhappy honourable gentleman had been trying in vain, for twenty-five years to precipitate William Barnacle into this—William Barnacle still put it to the House, and (at second-hand or so) to the country, whether he was to be precipitated into this. No matter that it was utterly irreconcilable with the nature of things and course of events, that the wretched honourable gentleman could possibly produce a Precedent for this—William Barnacle would nevertheless thank the honourable gentleman for that ironical cheer, and would close with him upon that issue, and would tell him to his teeth that there was NO precedent for this. It was not high wisdom, or the earth it bamboozled would never have been made, or, if made in a rash mistake, would have remained blank mud. But, Precedent and Precipitate together frightened all objection out of most people.

And there, too, was another Barnacle, a lively one, who had leaped through twenty places in quick succession, and was always in two or three at once, and who was the much-respected inventor of an art which he practised with great success and admiration in all Barnacle Governments. This was, when he was asked a Parliamentary question on any one topic, to return an answer on any other. It had done immense service, and brought him into high esteem with the Circumlocution Office.

And there, too, was a sprinkling of less distinguished Parliamentary Barnacles, who had not as yet got anything snug, and were going through their probation to prove their worthiness. These Barnacles perched upon staircases and hid in passages, waiting their orders to make houses or not to make houses; and they did all their hearing, and ohing, and cheering, and barking, under directions from the heads of the family; and they put dummy motions on the paper in the way of other men's motions; and they stalled disagreeable subjects off until late in the night and late in the session, and then with virtuous patriotism cried out that it was too late; and they went down into the country, whenever they were sent, and swore that Lord Decimus had revived trade from a swoon, and commerce from a fit, and had doubled the harvest of corn, quadrupled the harvest of hay, and prevented no end of gold from flying out of the Bank. Also these Barnacles were dealt, by the heads of the family, like so many cards below the court-cards, to public meetings and dinners; where they bore testimony to all sorts of services on the part of their noble and honourable relatives, and buttered the Barnacles on all sorts of toasts. And they stood, under similar orders, at all sorts of elections; and they turned out of their own seats, on the shortest notice and the most unreasonable terms, to let in other men; and they fetched and carried, and toadied and jobbed, and corrupted, and ate heaps of dirt, and were indefatigable in the public service. And there was not a list, in all the Circumlocution Office, of places that might fall vacant anywhere within half a century, from a lord of the Treasury to a Chinese consul, and up again to a governor-general of India, but, as applicants for such places, the names of some or of every one of these hungry and adhesive Barnacles were down.

Little Dorrit, ch. 34

The old device of abusive representation of incompetence in a grotesque form is here reduced to one phrase—'How not to do it'. Otherwise, Dickens' art is more restrained in detail, though no less violent in effect than was his attack on Bumble and the Board of Guardians. Realistic, rather than grotesque practices are assigned to these members of the ruling order; the sting of satire lies in an elaboration and repetition which reduces the whole to absurdity, without inviting the charge of misrepresentation or exaggeration in detail. The appropriate styles of the speakers in the House of Commons and Lords are parodied; the length of the passage gives a cumulative effect of suggesting that jobbery is endless, and pervades all areas of government and Civil Service: an effect aided by reference to the 'family' of Barnacles, with its hint of nepotism.

Grotesque caricature: black comedy

Dickens habitually used grotesque caricatures in his novels: sometimes for sheer comedy (Mrs. Gamp), sometimes as melodramatic villains (Quilp), sometimes for satirical purposes (Bumble, Mrs. Sparsit). But a sign of his increasing concern with the darker side of life is the grimmer material from which he fashioned the still very funny grotesques of his last novels. In early days, stage misers, conventional money-lenders, obvious hypocrites, and comically malevolent tooth-gnashers were his staple grotesque types. In his later books a less sociable association with death and corruption than that represented by undertakers (Mr. Sowerberry, Mr. Mould) was likely to inhere in the sources to which he turned for comic material.

After a street accident, Silas Wegg's leg was amputated, and then sold by a hospital porter to Mr. Venus, a taxidermist and articulator of skeletons. Now recovered, Wegg visits Venus in his shop.

24

Mr. Wegg, as an artful man who is sure of his supper

by-and-by, presses muffin on his host to soothe him into a compliant state of mind, or, as one might say, to grease his works. As the muffins disappear, little by little, the black shelves and nooks and corners begin to appear, and Mr. Wegg gradually acquires an imperfect notion that over against him on the chimney-piece is a Hindoo baby in a bottle, curved up with his big head tucked under him, as though he would instantly throw a summersault if the bottle were large enough.

When he deems Mr. Venus's wheels sufficiently lubricated, Mr. Wegg approaches his object by asking, as he lightly taps his hands together, to express an undesigning frame of mind :

'And how have I been going on, this long time, Mr. Venus?'

'Very bad,' says Mr. Venus, uncompromisingly.

'What? Am I still at home?' asks Mr. Wegg, with an air of surprise.

'Always at home.'

This would seem to be secretly agreeable to Wegg, but he veils his feelings, and observes, 'Strange. To what do you attribute it?'

'I don't know,' replies Venus, who is a haggard melancholy man, speaking in a weak voice of querulous complaint, 'to what to attribute it, Mr. Wegg. I can't work you into a miscellaneous one, nohow. Do what I will, you can't be got to fit. Anybody with a passable knowledge would pick you out at a look, and say— "No go! Don't match!"'

'Well, but hang it, Mr. Venus,' Wegg expostulates with some little irritation, 'that can't be personal and peculiar in *me*. It must often happen with miscellaneous ones.'

'With ribs (I grant you) always. But not else. When I prepare a miscellaneous one, I know beforehand that I can't keep to nature, and be miscellaneous with ribs, because every man has his own ribs, and no other man's will go with them; but elseways I can be miscellaneous. I have just sent home a Beauty—a perfect Beauty—to a school of art. One leg Belgian, one leg English, and the pickings of eight other people in it. Talk of not being qualified to be miscellaneous! By rights you *ought* to be, Mr. Wegg.'

Silas looks as hard at his one leg as he can in the dim light, and after a pause sulkily opines 'that it must be the fault of the other people. Or how do you mean to say it comes about?' he demands impatiently.

'I don't know how it comes about. Stand up a minute. Hold the light.' Mr. Venus takes from a corner by his chair, the bones of a leg and foot, beautifully pure, and put together with exquisite neatness. These he compares with Mr. Wegg's leg; that gentleman looking on, as if he were being measured for a riding-boot. 'No, I don't know how it is, but so it is. You have got a twist in that bone, to the best of my belief. *I* never saw the likes of you.'

Mr. Wegg having looked distrustfully at his own limb, and suspiciously at the pattern with which it had been compared, makes the point:

'I'll bet a pound that ain't an English one!'

'An easy wager, when we run so much into foreign! No, it belongs to that French gentleman.'

As he nods towards a point of darkness behind Mr. Wegg, the latter, with a slight start, looks round for 'that French gentleman,' whom he at length decries to be represented (in a very workmanlike manner) by his ribs only, standing on a shelf in another corner, like a piece of armour or a pair of stays.

'Oh!' says Mr. Wegg, with a sort of sense of being introduced; 'I dare say you were all right enough in your own country, but I hope no objections will be taken to my saying that the Frenchman was never yet born as I should wish to match.'

At this moment the greasy door is violently pushed inward, and a boy follows it, who says, after having let it slam:

'Come for the stuffed canary.'

'It's three and ninepence,' returns Venus; 'have you got the money?'

The boy produces four shillings. Mr. Venus, always in exceedingly low spirits, and making whimpering sounds, peers about for the stuffed canary. On his taking the candle to assist his search, Mr. Wegg observes that he has a convenient little shelf near his knees, exclusively appropriated to skeleton hands, which have very much the appearance of wanting to lay hold of him. From these Mr. Venus rescues the canary in a glass case, and shows it to the boy.

'There!' he whimpers. 'There's animation! On a twig, making up his mind to hop! Take care of him; he's a lovely specimen. —And three is four.'

The boy gathers up his change and has pulled the door open by a leather strap nailed to it for the purpose, when Venus cries out:

'Stop him! Come back, you young villain! You've got a tooth among them halfpence.'

'How was I to know I'd got it? You giv it me. I don't want none of your teeth. I've got enough of my own.' So the boy pipes as he selects it from his change, and throws it on the counter.

'Don't sauce *me* in the wicious pride of your youth,' Mr. Venus retorts pathetically. 'Don't hit *me* because you see I'm down. I'm low enough without that. It dropped into the till I suppose. They drop into everything. There was two in the coffee-pot at breakfast-time. Molars.'

'Very well, then,' argues the boy, 'what do you call names for?'

To which Mr. Venus only replies, shaking his shock of dusty hair, and winking his weak eyes, 'Don't sauce *me* in the wicious pride of your youth; don't hit *me* because I'm down. You've no idea how small you'd come out, if I had the articulating of you.'

This consideration seems to have its effect upon the boy, for he goes out grumbling.

'Oh dear me, dear me!' sighs Mr. Venus, heavily, snuffing the candle, 'the world that appeared so flowery has ceased to blow! You're casting your eye round the shop,

Mr. Wegg. Let me show you a light. My working bench.
My young man's bench. A Wice. Tools. Bones, warious.
Preserved Indian baby. African ditto. Bottled preparations,
warious. Everything within reach of your hand, in good
preservation. The mouldy ones a-top. What's in those
hampers over them again, I don't quite remember. Say,
human, warious. Cats. Articulated English baby. Dogs.
Ducks. Glass eyes, warious. Mummied bird. Dried cuticle,
warious. Oh dear me! That's the general panoramic view.'
Our Mutual Friend, Bk. 1, ch. 7

The taxidermist and articulator of skeletons, and the
one-legged man whose amputated limb he has bought,
are simply a pair of comic rogues. They are later to display
an avarice and engage in a conspiracy which underlines
one theme of the book; but essentially they introduce low
comic relief in a novel whose scope is remarkably wide.

But their comedy is comedy of horror and disgust.
Bones are funny in themselves; the dehumanized remains
of humanity are incongruously related to the full humanity
('that French gentleman') of which they were once a
part. Nausea is invited— 'The mouldy ones atop' (mouldy
what?), 'Dried cuticle, warious"—in order that a laughter
of relief (that our lives are not filled with such things)
may be forced from us.

Dickens' gift for verbal comedy is still used: note the
absurdity of Mr. Venus's rather poetic diction when contrasted with his trade. And Dickens' imagination seems to
create new horrors in the recesses of the shop effortlessly.
But horrors they are: the grisly laughter here must be
associated with the similar figures of Jerry Cruncher, the
comic grave-robber of *A Tale of Two Cities*, or the tide-
way jack of *Great Expectations* who dresses in the clothes
of drowned and washed-up corpses.

F. R. Leavis, while fully recognising Dickens' classic standing, excluded him from *The Great Tradition* on the grounds that the great line of serious English novelists could not contain this 'classic of entertainment'. Most critics no longer agree that Dicken's permanent concern with the amusement of his audience can justify his omission, even from a line headed by writers so overtly serious as George Eliot and Henry James. The old label of 'entertainer' is seldom used sneeringly to dismiss Dickens nowadays, although certain of his weaknesses—notably his *penchant* for melodrama and an oversimple presentation of the confrontation of good and evil—do seem to spring from too heavy a dependance on the accepted standards of popular entertainment as exemplified in the theatres he loved.

But Dickens' sturdy sense of his own worth would probably not have led him to discard the title. Entertaining audiences, in amateur theatricals during his prime, and in the public readings from his writings which severely taxed his nervous system, and contributed to his death, was with him a passion. And his ability to entertain was as surely a part of his art as his serious concern with humanity and right conduct. The techniques of comedy and irony in prose have been permanently enriched by his awareness that readers had to be persuaded before they would be content to accept a message, and in his late, 'serious' novels, as in his early comedies, he found, and will continue to find, readers who recognise that the artist's sense of life, and the writer's sense of language are enhanced by coming to us through the man's sense of absurdity and fun.

Reference list of Dickens' works

Novels

Note: The dates given are the dates of first publication in volume form. Most of Dickens' novels were published in separate monthly parts. *Oliver Twist* ran as a monthly serial in *Bentley's Miscellany*, and *The Old Curiosity Shop* and *Barnaby Rudge* in *Master Humphrey's Clock*. The three novels which did not appear monthly, appeared in weekly parts: *Hard Times* in *Household Words*, and *A Tale of Two Cities* and *Great Expectations* in *All the Year Round*.

The Posthumous Papers of the Pickwick Club, containing a faithful record of the perambulations, perils, travels, adventures, and sporting transactions of the corresponding members. Edited by 'Boz'. (1837)

Oliver Twist; or, the parish boy's progress (1838), ed. Kathleen Tillotson, Clarendon Press, Oxford. 1966.

The Life and Adventures of Nicholas Nickleby: containing a faithful account of the fortunes, misfortunes, uprisings, downfallings, and complete career of the Nickleby family (1839)

The Old Curiosity Shop (1841)

Barnaby Rudge: a tale of the riots of 'eighty (1841)

The Life and Adventures of Martin Chuzzlewit: his relatives, friends, and enemies. Comprising all his wiles and his ways, with an historical record of what he did, and what he didn't; showing, moreover, who inherited the family plate, who came in for the silver spoons, and who for the wooden ladles. This whole forming a complete key to the house of Chuzzlewit (1844)

Dealings with the Firm of Dombey and Son, Wholesale, Retail, and for Exportation (1848)

REFERENCE LIST OF DICKENS' WORKS

The Personal History, Adventures, Experiences, and Observation of David Copperfield the Younger of Bluderstone Rookery (Which he never meant to be published on any account) (1850)
Bleak House (1853)
Hard Times: For these times (1854)
Little Dorrit (1857)
A Tale of Two Cities (1859)
Great Expectations (1861)
Our Mutual Friend (1865)
The Mystery of Edwin Drood (Unfinished) (1870)
Note: The *Sketches, American Notes, Christmas Books, Pictures from Italy, Christmas Stories, Child's History, Reprinted Pieces,* and *Uncommercial Traveller* are normally standard volumes, or half volumes in editions of Dickens collected works. (The only one at present in print is the *Oxford Illustrated Dickens*, O.U.P., London New York and Toronto). Other material may be harder to find. The fullest edition of Dickens' works is *The Centenary Edition of the Works of Charles Dickens*, Chapman & Hall, London: Charles Scribner's sons, New York, 1911.

Other Works

The Nonesuch Dickens, ed. A. Waugh, H. Walpole, W. Dexter and T. Hatton, Nonesuch Press, London 1937. (Includes *The Letters of Charles Dickens*, 3 vols., ed. Walter Dexter.)
The Letters of Charles Dickens, ed. M. House and G. Storey, (*The Pilgrim Edition*), Clarendon Press, Oxford. Vol. i., 1965. Further vols. in preparation.
The Speeches of Charles Dickens, ed. K. J. Fielding, Clarendon Press, Oxford, 1960.

Bibliography

BUTT, J. and TILLOTSON, K., *Dickens at Work*, Methuen, London, Essential Books, Fair Lawn, N.J., 1957. Study of Dickens' corrections and planning from his work-papers.

CHESTERTON, G. K., *Charles Dickens* (1906), Methuen, London, 1956. General survey; the jolly Dickens.

CHESTERTON, G. K., *Appreciations and Criticisms of the Works of Charles Dickens*, John Dent, London, 1911. The introductions for the Everyman editions of the novels.

COCKSHUT, A. O. J., *The Imagination of Charles Dickens*, Collins, London, 1961. Stimulating critical study.

COLLINS, PHILIP, *Dickens and Crime*, Macmillan, London, St. Martin's Press, New York, 1962. Informative study of Dickens' attitudes and opinions in the light of nineteenth-century penology.

COLLINS, PHILIP, *Dickens and Education*, Macmillan, London, St. Martin's Press, New York, 1963. Similar study to above.

DAVIS, EARLE, *The Flint and the Flame: The Artistry of Charles Dickens*, University of Missouri Press, Columbia, Miss., Victor Gollancz, London 1963. Critical study of Dicken's development and contemporary sources. Informative, often stimulating; a few howlers.

FIELDING, K. J., *Charles Dickens*, Longman's Green and Co., London, for the British Council, 1953, revised 1963. Superb guide through mass of material on Dickens. Certainly one of the best of the Writers and their Work series. Excellent bibliography.

FIELDING, K. J., *Charles Dickens, a Critical Introduction*, Longman's Green and Co., London and New York, 1957. Useful general study.

118

FORD, G. H., *Dickens and His Readers: Aspects of Novel-Criticism since 1836*, Princeton U.P., N.J., 1955, Oldbourne Press, London, 1965. Very important examination of public and critical responses to Dickens from *Pickwick* to the present day.

FORD, G. H. and LANE, L., (ed.) *The Dickens Critics*, Cornell U.P., Ithaca, N.Y., 1961. Essential collection of the most important essays and studies of Dickens from Poe to Angus Wilson.

FORSTER, J., *The Life of Charles Dickens*, Chapman & Hall, London, 1872-74. The authorised life by Dickens' oldest friend. In spite of respect for decorum, remains essential source of first-hand information.

GARIS, R., *The Dickens Theatre: A Reassessment of the Novels*, Clarendon Press, Oxford, 1965. Stimulating examination of the novels in the light of theatrical conventions.

GISSING, G., *Charles Dickens: A Critical Study*, Cecil Palmer, London, 1898. Important early general study by realist admirer.

GISSING, G., *The Immortal Dickens*, Cecil Palmer, London, 1925. Introductions to unfinished Rochester edition.

GROSS, J. and PEARSON, G., *Dickens and the Twentieth Century*, Routledge & Kegan Paul, London, University of Toronto Press, Toronto, 1962. Interesting collection of new essays, mainly on the individual novels.

HOUSE, H., *The Dickens World*, Oxford University Press, London and New York, 1941. Pioneer study of Dickens' social attitudes in a background of fact, rather than popular tradition.

JOHNSON, E., *Charles Dickens, His Tragedy and Triumph*, New York, Victor Gollancz, London, 1953. Now the standard life. Full and readable.

MARCUS, S., *Dickens from Pickwick to Dombey*, Chatto & Windus, London, 1965. Critical study of the first seven novels.

MILLER, J. H., *Charles Dickens: The World of his Novels*, Harvard U.P., Cambridge, Mass., Oxford U.P., London, 1958. Interesting application of thematic criticism to Dickens, arguing for a unified moral and aesthetic vision in each of the novels.

PHILLIPS, W. C., *Dickens, Reade, and Collins, Sensation Novelists: A study in the conditions and theories of novel writing in Victorian England*, (1918), Russell & Russell, New York, 1962. Interesting examination of an important aspect of the work of Dickens and his lesser associates.

STOEHR, T., *Dickens; The Dreamer's Stance*, Cornell U.P., Ithaca, N.Y., 1965. Stimulating examination of some of the psychological implications of parts of Dickens' writing